AF679038

# Global Diaspora Politics and Social Movements:

## Emerging Research and Opportunities

Emily B. Stacey
*Swansea University, UK*

A volume in the Advances in Religious and Cultural Studies (ARCS) Book Series

IGI Global
DISSEMINATOR OF KNOWLEDGE

Published in the United States of America by
IGI Global
Information Science Reference (an imprint of IGI Global)
701 E. Chocolate Avenue
Hershey PA, USA 17033
Tel: 717-533-8845
Fax: 717-533-8661
E-mail: cust@igi-global.com
Web site: http://www.igi-global.com

Copyright © 2019 by IGI Global. All rights reserved. No part of this publication may be reproduced, stored or distributed in any form or by any means, electronic or mechanical, including photocopying, without written permission from the publisher.
Product or company names used in this set are for identification purposes only. Inclusion of the names of the products or companies does not indicate a claim of ownership by IGI Global of the trademark or registered trademark.

Library of Congress Cataloging-in-Publication Data

Names: Stacey, Emily, 1984- author.
Title: Global diaspora politics and social movements : emerging research and opportunities / by Emily B. Stacey.
Description: Hershey : Information Science Reference, [2018]
Identifiers: LCCN 2018035052| ISBN 9781522577577 (hardcover) | ISBN 9781522577584 (ebook)
Subjects: LCSH: Social movements. | Feminism--Political aspects. | Sex role--Political aspects.
Classification: LCC HM881 .S7233 2018 | DDC 303.48/4--dc23 LC record available at https://lccn.loc.gov/2018035052

This book is published in the IGI Global book series Advances in Religious and Cultural Studies (ARCS) (ISSN: 2475-675X; eISSN: 2475-6768)

British Cataloguing in Publication Data
A Cataloguing in Publication record for this book is available from the British Library.

All work contributed to this book is new, previously-unpublished material.
The views expressed in this book are those of the authors, but not necessarily of the publisher.

For electronic access to this publication, please contact: eresources@igi-global.com.

# Advances in Religious and Cultural Studies (ARCS) Book Series

ISSN:2475-675X
EISSN:2475-6768

Editor-in-Chief: Nancy Erbe, California State University-Dominguez Hills, USA

## MISSION

In the era of globalization, the diversity of the world and various cultures becomes apparent as cross-cultural interactions turn into a daily occurrence for individuals in all professions. Understanding these differences is necessary in order to promote effective partnerships and interactions between those from different religious and cultural backgrounds.

The **Advances in Religious and Cultural Studies (ARCS)** book series brings together a collection of scholarly publications on topics pertaining to religious beliefs, culture, population studies, and sociology. Books published within this series are ideal for professionals, theorists, researchers, and students seeking the latest research on collective human behavior in terms of religion, social structure, and cultural identity and practice.

## COVERAGE

- Globalization and Culture
- Human Rights and Ethics
- Politics and Religion
- Impact of Religion on Society
- Gender
- Social Stratification and Classes
- Cultural Identity
- Cross-Cultural Interaction
- Sociology
- Cults and Religious Movements

IGI Global is currently accepting manuscripts for publication within this series. To submit a proposal for a volume in this series, please contact our Acquisition Editors at Acquisitions@igi-global.com or visit: http://www.igi-global.com/publish/.

The Advances in Religious and Cultural Studies (ARCS) Book Series (ISSN 2475-675X) is published by IGI Global, 701 E. Chocolate Avenue, Hershey, PA 17033-1240, USA, www.igi-global.com. This series is composed of titles available for purchase individually; each title is edited to be contextually exclusive from any other title within the series. For pricing and ordering information please visit http://www.igi-global.com/book-series/advances-religious-cultural-studies/84269. Postmaster: Send all address changes to above address. ©© 2019 IGI Global. All rights, including translation in other languages reserved by the publisher. No part of this series may be reproduced or used in any form or by any means – graphics, electronic, or mechanical, including photocopying, recording, taping, or information and retrieval systems – without written permission from the publisher, except for non commercial, educational use, including classroom teaching purposes. The views expressed in this series are those of the authors, but not necessarily of IGI Global.

## Titles in this Series

*For a list of additional titles in this series, please visit:*
*https://www.igi-global.com/book-series/advances-religious-cultural-studies/84269*

***Infocommunication Skills as a Rehabilitation and Social Reintegration Tool for Inmates***
Lídia Oliveira (University of Aveiro, Portugal) and Daniela Graça (University of Aveiro, Portugal)
Information Science Reference • ©2019 • 326pp • H/C (ISBN: 9781522559757) • US $175.00

***Post-Holocaust Studies in a Modern Context***
Nitza Davidovitch (Ariel University, Israel) Ronen A. Cohen (Ariel University, Israel) and Eyal Lewin (Ariel University Israel)
Information Science Reference • ©2019 • 286pp • H/C (ISBN: 9781522562580) • US $185.00

***Handbook of Research on Heritage Management and Preservation***
Patrick Ngulube (University of South Africa, South Africa)
Information Science Reference • ©2018 • 508pp • H/C (ISBN: 9781522531371) • US $265.00

***Redefining Translation and Interpretation in Cultural Evolution***
Olaf Immanuel Seel (Ionian University of Corfu, Greece)
Information Science Reference • ©2018 • 310pp • H/C (ISBN: 9781522528326) • US $195.00

***Educational Development and Infrastructure for Immigrants and Refugees***
Şefika Şule Erçetin (Lancaster University, UK & Hacettepe University, Turkey)
Information Science Reference • ©2018 • 375pp • H/C (ISBN: 9781522533252) • US $195.00

***Social Considerations of Migration Movements and Immigration Policies***
Şefika Şule Erçetin (Lancaster University, UK & Hacettepe University, Turkey)
Information Science Reference • ©2018 • 283pp • H/C (ISBN: 9781522533221) • US $195.00

***Global Ideologies Surrounding Children's Rights and Social Justice***
Icarbord Tshabangu (Leeds Trinity University, UK)
Information Science Reference • ©2018 • 296pp • H/C (ISBN: 9781522525783) • US $195.00

*For an entire list of titles in this series, please visit:*
*https://www.igi-global.com/book-series/advances-religious-cultural-studies/84269*

IGI Global
DISSEMINATOR OF KNOWLEDGE

701 East Chocolate Avenue, Hershey, PA 17033, USA
Tel: 717-533-8845 x100 • Fax: 717-533-8661
E-Mail: cust@igi-global.com • www.igi-global.com

# Table of Contents

# Preface

Global politics has transformed in recent years, with shifts inward by some of the most important actors due to a rise in nationalist ideology, the breakdown of multiple societies, and even nation-state legitimacy with the civil war in Syria that devolved into a multi-national crisis with the Islamic State. The nation-state, arguably, has been in question for much of the digital age, as citizens become transnational and claim loyalty to many different groups, causes, and in some cases, states. The displacement of stateless groups has long been part and parcel of the development of civilization. Although diasporic politics has been most commonly associated with Jewish displacement and resettlement dating back to World War II, there are numerous other groups in contemporary politics that represent diasporic communities, both in terms of territory (or the existence of a nation-state) or more psychological aspects of diaspora (feelings of exclusion from mainstream society, isolation). Contemporary diaspora (starting in the 20$^{th}$ century) and the politics that accompanies diasporic communities have become increasingly important focal points of comparative and political science research. Gamlen et al. (2017) note that in the contemporary international community, more than half of the world's countries have established diasporic communities or organizations that are interacting with emigrants and their families. Demmers (2002) provides four explanations as to the increased emphasis on diaspora politics, "(1) the rise of a new pattern of conflict; (2) the rapid rise of war refugees; (3) the increased speed of communication and mobility; and (4) the increased production of cultural and political boundaries" (p. 86).

According to Anthias (1998), "Diaspora [contemporary/new diaspora] references a connection between groups across different nation-states whose commonality derives from an original but maybe removed homeland; a new identity becomes constructed on a world scale, which crosses national borders and boundaries" (p. 559), which provides for (arguably) easier construction of a collective identity. Due to the shifting of the world order and power dynamics in the international community, "The significance of diasporic identity lies in its force as a symbolic declaration of liberation from the abject position of 'ethnic minority' in 'an oppressive national hegemony'" (Clifford, 1994, p. 255). The concept and perception of identity is in constant flux, which alters the concept of "diaspora space," or the examination of the "intersections of diaspora and the resulting hybrid identities" (Nititham, 2008, p. 70). Yet as Brubaker (2005) argues the inclusion of different aspects of diaspora under the 'let a thousand diasporas arise' approach leads to a fundamental misunderstanding or misdiagnosis of diaspora, with the rise of digital, queer, or female diaspora. However, Brubaker adheres to the more classically accepted definition of diaspora as related to a territorial displacement and longing for that homeland, rather than in a modern conception of diaspora as affective, sentimental, or psychological. In the manner of Sökefeld (2006), "It is difficult conceptually to separate diaspora as social form from diaspora as a type of consciousness" (p. 265), and as such this work focuses on both the territorial definition, but places increased emphasis on the psychological conception of diaspora as well.

Adamson and Demtriou's (2007) definition of diaspora is used as the basis of identifying diaspora in this work, which describes diaspora as a social collectivity that exists across borders and has 1) sustained a collective national, cultural, or religious identity via lasting connection to a homeland (real or imagined); and 2) has established and maintained a network that is able to serve the interests of the diasporic community members. This definition becomes critical to the mobilization of diasporic communities for sociopolitical change, which is highlighted in the case studies in this work. Koinova (2016) describes diaspora mobilization as "individual and collective actions of identity-based social entrepreneurs who organize and encourage migrants to behave in a concerted way to make homeland-oriented claims, bring about a political objective, or contribute to a cause" (p. 501). What is important to emphasize here is the necessity to cultivate a shared (or collective) identity, this is critical to both diasporic and social movements alike, however, the identity does tend to be more fixed when analyzing diasporic mobilization as it tends to be centered on an ethnic group, religion, language, or place of origin. Hall, who is a prominent figure in diaspora studies for his inclusion of race and ethnicity in the construction of a diasporic identity or consciousness, argues from the perspective of a native-born Jamaican man living in the U.K. and highlights the concept of cultural identity construction. Hall (1990) articulates diasporic cultural identity, asserting:

*The diaspora experience as I intend it here, is defined, not be essence or purity, but by the recognition of a necessary heterogeneity and diversity; by a conception of 'identity' which lives with and through, not despite, difference; by hybridity. Diaspora identities are those which are constantly producing and reproducing themselves anew, through transformation and difference. (p. 235)*

Nititham highlights the existence of the global citizen with transnational identities, as opposed to the traditional nation-state conception of what constitutes a citizen (such as adherence to a common language or shared cultural norms), which is discussed further in Chapter One. Conquergood (1991) reiterates the construction of identity as being "invented and contingent, not autonomous: 'I' is therefore, not a unified subject, a fixed identity, or that solid mass covered with layers of superficialities one has gradually to peel off before one can see its true face" (p. 184). This is particularly true in the digital age where borders and boundaries that once separated cultures, religions, and civilizations are becoming intertwined and *glocalized* via the shared proliferation of digital tools, such as the internet and social media platforms. Meyrowitz (1985) foreshadows the changing structure of the diasporic identity with the proliferation of new media technologies, writing:

*While we tend to think of our group affiliations simply in terms who we are, our sense of identity is also shaped by where we are and who is with us. A change in the structure of situations – as a result of changes in media or other factors – will change people's sense of us and them [emphasis added by author]. An important issue to consider in predicting the effects of the new media on group identities is how the new medium alters who shares social information with whom. As social information-systems merge or divide, so will group identities. (p. 54)*

Yau (2007) notes, "Identity at home and away is vital in locating ourselves in the world" (p. 48), although it is crucial to reiterate that the contemporary conception of identity can span nations, religions, gender, and sometimes ethnicity (see the Rachel Dolezal story). Traditional signifiers of identity (particularly national) have become blurred, which will likely lead to an increase in research on diasporic sentiments and politics in the realm of psychology and affect.

Ong (2003) characterizes the contemporary definition of diaspora as "refer[ing] not to permanent exile, but rather to the global imaginary invoked by transnational subjects located in metropolitan centers who wish to exercise a new form of power through the use of informational technology" (p. 86). Vertovec (2005) reiterates the importance of considering digital technologies when examining contemporary diasporic communities and their ability to create change, noting, "New communication technologies have improved abilities to mobilize, and multiculturalism policies in receiving countries have revitalized ethnic pride and assertiveness" (p. 1). This is, of course, before the wave of nationalism that has impacted the international community with major actors such as the United States (post-Trump election) and the United Kingdom (post-Brexit) turning inward with their politics, and using the politics of Othering to justify retreating from the global stage. Werbner (1997) highlights the counterintuitive nature nation-states (such as the United States) implementing policies that vilify a diasporic community that enable that community to mobilize dissent and the negotiations that are involved on the part of the diaspora in terms of host politics that may be hostile to their existence and the politics of belonging. Werbner (1997) states:

*The argument about ethnic naming highlights the fact that it is not only Western representations of the Other which essentialize. In their performative rhetoric the people we study essentialize their imagined communities in order to mobilize action. Within the spaces of civil society, the politics of ethnicity in Britain [or arguably other Western nations] are not so much imposed as grounded in essentialist self-imaginings of community. Hence, ethnic leaders essentialize communal identities in their competition for state grants [funding] and formal leadership positions. But – equally importantly – such leaders narrate and argue over these identities in the social spaces, which they themselves have created, far from the public eye.*

However, this same nationalism that often uses diasporic communities as scapegoats for crime and other nefarious deeds within a society, could explain why the world is witnessing resurgence in diasporic politics and marginalized populations creating awareness of their struggles. Demmers (2002) argues, "Due to the increased production of cultural and political boundaries in countries of the Western world, contemporary diaspora have found full incorporation in the countries in the West within which they resettle either not possible or not desirable" (p. 88). While Delano and Gamlen (2014) assert that it is possible that when states incorporate immigration (diaspora) policies that prioritize some over others, it can exacerbate preexisting divisions based along lines of race, class, gender, ethnic origin, etc. Often, Joppke (2005) argues, "embracing the emigrant" is synonymous with "bashing of the immigrant," and "bears the unmistakable signatures of the political Right" (p. 243). The pervasive nationalist ideologies spreading across the international community have publicly utilized anti-immigrant sentiment to stoke base tensions and solidify voters around rights for *us* rather than *them* (see Stacey, 2018).

This work explores the ever-developing concept of diaspora, which at the very least requires an emotional attachment to a collective origin and shared cultural identity that transcends living in the homeland (Vertovec, 2005). The feeling of attachment to a homeland and the willingness to mobilize for it typically is dependent on the situation within the homeland (whether real or imagined); events such as natural disasters, regime change, or intimate policy decisions (e.g., 2018 Irish referendum) can stir not just sentiment but sociopolitical action. The work will first introduce the concept of diaspora and the evolving literature on diaspora politics; the second chapter will relate diaspora and social movement literature in establishing the main thesis of this work, which is explaining how contemporary diasporic communities are mobilizing and their effectiveness; chapter three focuses on methodological considerations and provides a brief explanation of the case studies; and in-depth analyses of the cases chosen, which focus on two theoretical considerations of diaspora (traditional, or territorial; and psychological). The case study on the psychological elements of diaspora emphasizes gender diaspora, and uses primary source interviews to provide a more intimate description of what it means to live in a diasporic community within the United States.

Stuart Hall (1990) argues fundamentally diaspora members carry a consciousness that makes them acutely aware of differences, and that consciousness transforms into diasporic identity by recognizing (perhaps celebrating) difference rather than assimilate. This consciousness is a critical aspect to mobilizing contemporary diasporic communities into sociopolitical movements for change. It is an awareness of the past, the homeland, origins, and an acutely intimate experience of living resettlement, whether in an entirely new land or attempting self-determination in ancestral lands. Diaspora politics (as a field of study) analyzes the political actions and behaviors of transnational ethnic communities and the relationship between the homeland (place of origin) and host land (place of emigration; King & Melvin, 1999/2000). Diaspora politics have become increasingly critical to various issues that plague the international community and move beyond the state apparatus. As

Gamlen et al. (2017) note, diasporic politics are becoming less state-centered as diasporic and transnational organizations (that are often aided by digital tools) are fostering community and political action within the diaspora. According to Alonso and Mylonas (2017), "Sub-state actors' motivations and objectives in relation to diaspora groups are formed separately from state policies and institutions, which on occasion lead to more positive reactions from the populations that they target" (p. 6). Diasporic organizations may include political interest groups (or lobbies) and other such advocacy groups, religious associations (which are critical to the case study on psychological diaspora presented later in this work), education and cultural programs, social groups, and youth organizations (which help foster a sense of the homeland within the host society; Dickinson, 2015; Gamlen, 2008; Werbner, 2002). The divorcing diaspora politics from the state and providing for community organizations that support the causes of the transnational population, arguably provides those diasporic organizations more legitimacy than if they had been formed and advocated by the state (particularly the host state). The politics of diaspora differ based on the shared consciousness of the diasporic community; yet a basic assumption of diaspora is that the community remains oriented to a collective identity. Diaspora is a transnational concept because they not only maintain ties to the homeland (place of origin) but are actively involved in the host state's politics, society, economy, and culture, which allows for the fostering of strong bonds with the host society.

This work will focus on global diaspora politics (and collective identity maintenance) from a territorial (traditional) as well as psychological (contemporary) perspective and contemporary social movements within the diaspora. The purpose of this work is to promote a broader definition of diaspora than the traditional definition provides for, in that affective and psychological considerations also come into play when analyzing diaspora politics and organizations. This work is not exhaustive in analyzing the field of diaspora studies, but provides traditional and contemporary cases for analysis. For a complete and comprehensive study of diaspora politics, one would need to consult a multitude of literature over the course of decades, which is not the purpose of this work. The author wanted to paint a clear picture of contemporary diaspora politics and the communities that foster around diasporic issues, and often create social movements from diasporic engagement. While there are numerous diasporic communities that could have been included in this work, the cases chosen highlight the territorial versus psychological nature of contemporary diaspora politics (the Kurds and the female diaspora).

## REFERENCES

Adamson, F., & Demetriou, M. (2007). Remapping the Boundaries of 'State' and 'National Identity': Incorporating Diasporas into IR Theorizing. *European Journal of International Relations*, *13*(4), 489–526. doi:10.1177/1354066107083145

Anthias, F. (1998). Evaluating Diaspora: Beyond Ethnicity? *Sociology*, *32*(3), 557–580.

Brah, A. (1996). *Cartographies of Diaspora*. New York: Routledge.

Clifford, J. (1994). Diasporas. *Cultural Anthropology,* (9), 302-38.

Conquergood, D. (1991). Rethinking ethnography: Towards a critical cultural politics. *Communication Monographs*, *58*(2), 179–194. doi:10.1080/03637759109376222

Délano, A., & Gamlen, A. (2014). Comparing and Theorizing State–diaspora Relations. *Political Geography*, *41*, 43–53. doi:10.1016/j.polgeo.2014.05.005

Demmers, J. (2002). Diaspora and Conflict: Locality, Long-Distance Nationalism, and Delocalization of Conflict Dynamics. *The Public*, *9*(1), 85–96.

Gamlen, A., Cummings, M., & Vaaler, P. (2017). Explaining the Rise of Diaspora Institutions. *Journal of Ethnic and Migration Studies*, 1–25. doi:10.1080/1369183X.2017.1409163

Hall, S. (1990). Cultural identity and diaspora. In J. Rutherford (Ed.), *Identity: Community, Culture, Difference* (pp. 222–237). London: Lawrence & Wishart.

Joppke, C. (2005). *Selecting by Origin: Ethnic Migration in the Liberal State*. Cambridge, MA: Harvard University Press.

Koinova, M. (2016). Sustained vs. episodic mobilization among conflict-generated diasporas. *International Political Science Review*, *37*(4), 500–516. doi:10.1177/0192512115591641

Meyrowitz, M. (1985). *No Sense of Place*. Oxford, UK: Oxford University Press.

Nititham, D. S. (2008). Locating the self in diaspora space. T*ranslocations: The Irish Migration. Race and Social Transformation Review*, *3*(1), 1–17.

Ong, A. (2003). Cyberpublics and Diaspora politics among transnational Chinese. *Interventions*, *5*(1), 82–100. doi:10.1080/1369803200049815

Stacey, E. (2018). *Nationalism, Social Movements, and Activism: Emerging Research and Opportunities*. IGI Global. doi:10.4018/978-1-5225-5433-2

Vertovec, S. (2005). *The Political Importance of Diaspora*. The Center on Migration, Policy, and Society. Working Paper No. 13, University of Oxford.

Werbner, P. (1997). Introduction: the dialectics of cultural hybridity. In P. Werbner & T. Modood (Eds.), *Debating Cultural Hybridity* (pp. 1–26). London: Zed Books.

Yau, N. (2007). Celtic Tiger, Hidden Dragon: Exploring identity among second generation Chinese in Ireland. *Translocations*, *2*(1), 48–69.

# Introduction

This work examines contemporary global diaspora politics and the social/political movements that diasporic communities are establishing to fight for increased rights as well as recognition in both host and home countries. The work analyzes two conceptions of diaspora, the traditional notion of diaspora, which is characterized by boundaries, borders, national identity, and citizenship based on place of origin. The traditional diaspora politics is highlighted in Chapter Five with a focus on the struggle of the Kurds to self-determine and establish a sovereign, autonomous homeland in the current global political environment. The second conception of diaspora is linked to psychological or affective aspects of belonging and the experiences of members of the American Muslim diaspora. The affective diaspora is examined via gender politics and through the international women's movements occurring in 2017-18. The work emphasizes varied definitions of diaspora that transcend that of borders and national identity based citizenship, to the transnational global community that exists today.

# Chapter 1
# Citizenship and Diasporic Politics:
## A Brief Introduction


## ABSTRACT

*This chapter introduces readers to classical and contemporary definitions of citizenship, the development of the nation-state, and the concept of national identity as well as other forms of identity construction. The chapter also focuses on diaspora literature and introducing the classical and contemporary characterizations of diaspora and theories on diaspora politics. Concepts such as hybridity and transnationalism are briefly presented as these concepts feed into the contemporary definitions of diaspora, which are less focused on a place of origin or homeland attachment. The chapter also delves into the Othering of national politics toward diasporic communities, providing examples from recent American policy.*


## INTRODUCTION

The concept of citizenship has certainly been tested in the 21st century and development of the transnational state, with available technologies increasingly blurring the boundaries of nation-states, governance, influence, and what it means to belong or the concept of *home*. Citizenship, in the broadest international relations terms, is belonging (legally and politically) to a state and was a byproduct of establishment and proliferation of the nation-state

DOI: 10.4018/978-1-5225-7757-7.ch001

Copyright © 2019, IGI Global. Copying or distributing in print or electronic forms without written permission of IGI Global is prohibited.

as the legitimate form of government (and arguably, the most fair division of previously occupied lands). With the French Revolution the idea of the nation-state, a politically organized area in which a nation and state occupy the same space, became the aspiration of political elites around the world. The idea that the map of states should look like a map of nations was consciously promoted by European philosophers and elites, who viewed the opportunity to create the map as a way of controlling the sovereignty and territorial integrity of states after the fall of the monarchies in Europe. The problem for these elites was that nation-states, or well-defined, stable nations living within distinct boundaries, were an ideal that didn't actually exist. Nations are created, not born of some specific ancestral group.

Since nation-states, thought necessary to maintain the territorial integrity of the states of Europe, did not really exist, they had to be created. In some cases, this meant privileging one ethnic at the expense of others. In other cases, it meant absorbing smaller entities into their borders. It often meant redrawing national borders to fit nations, most often determined by language. But mostly the creation of nation-states took the form of an explicit attempt by elites to create a single national identity out of the diverse peoples within their borders. They did this by promoting a sense of shared history and culture (whether based in fact or not) through public education, and through the promotion of national languages and alphabets, symbols, holidays, songs, and dress. As Nititham argues, "Assumptions about an entire nationality, a minority ethnic group or a categorization of people are not just linked to people's individual thoughts; these reflect a collective history and the popular imagination. The power and value placed upon these adjectives gives them real meaning, sometimes with joyful memories, in other cases, painful ones" (2008, P. 74).

The first political organization of states based on the ideas of territoriality and sovereignty date back to the early city-states of the Fertile Crescent. The philosophical origins of the modern state begin already with the Peace of Westphalia in 1648. The concept of the nation-state and nationalism took hold in Europe in the nineteenth century and was exported around the world through European colonization. Even so, the modern concept of state grew very slowly at first and has expanded rapidly only very recently. As of the time of the Declaration of Independence, there were only some thirty-five empires, kingdoms, and countries in the entire world. By the beginning of WWII, that number had only doubled to around seventy. Following WWII, many former European colonies, finally achieved independence and consciously choose to retain their colonial borders, languages, and the very concept of statehood itself as a way of avoiding territorial and ethnic conflicts that might otherwise have torn these newly independent states apart. Kalra, Kalhon, and Hutynuk (2005, P. 35) note, "Indeed, for much of the formerly colonized world, the role of nation-states as a key determinant of social identity and as the main mechanism for enhancing and promoting social identity is relatively weak when considered against expressive cultural ties (music, film, faith, etc.)." In reality, the nation-state has not been comprised of pure ethnicities or a singular national identity. This is due to the tendency of humans to migrate and marry (and procreate) outside of their ethnic/national identity; rarely in the international community has an ethnically homogenous, even though numerous leaders throughout history have attempted to cleanse various countries of non-native identities (Karim, 2002). Georgiou (2014, P. 85) asserts, "The nation-state aims to sustain its power and legitimacy based on ideologies of singularity – of singular loyalties, of the singularity of the national

territorial ownership and boundedness." Yet new (transnational) diaspora and diasporic communities are less bound to a place of origin and increasingly recognizing cultural, heritage-based, and racial identities in relation to diaspora instead of the vehement adherence to the concept of a homeland.

Cultural and heritage-based expression is extremely important in diasporic communities seeking to maintain a semblance of a connection to the homeland and their ancestors. These diasporic communities have lent traditions, food, faith, and ideals to Western countries, and have certainly challenged the traditional conception of a singular national identity. Ganguly eloquently summarizes the importance of affective or sentimental attachment that characterizes diaspora consciousness or identity construction,

*Recollections of the past serve as the active ideological terrain on which people represent themselves to themselves. The past acquires a more marked salience with subjects for whom categories of the present have been made unusually unstable or unpredictable, as a consequence of the displacement enforced by postcolonial and migrant circumstances. (1992, P. 29)*

With the creation of newly independent countries, the number of states increased dramatically. In the forty years following 1945, some ninety African and Asian states were admitted to the United Nations. By 1990, independent states totaled 180, and their number increased again following the disintegration in the 1990s of the USSR, Yugoslavia, and Czechoslovakia, which created more than twenty new countries where only three had existed before. With the admittance of South Sudan in July of 2011, the number of member states of the United Nations stands, as of this writing, at 193. The establishment of borders and distinct, distinguishable nationalities was an important feature of the traditional international community post-Westphalia. Anzaldua articulates the issues with the concept of borders (early in the digital age) arguing, "Borders are set up to define the places that are safe and unsafe to distinguish us from them. A border is a dividing line, a narrow strip along a steep edge. A borderland is vague and undetermined place created by the emotional reside of an unnatural boundary. It is in a constant state of transition. The prohibited and forbidden are its inhabitants" (1987, P. 25). As Ang (2003, P. 3) asserts, "the limits of diaspora lie precisely in its own assumed boundedness, its inevitable tendency to stress its internal coherence and unity, logically set apart from *others*. Diasporic formations transgress the boundaries of the nation-state on behalf of a globally dispersed *people...*" [emphasis added by author]. This book regards the people who sit in at the intersection of inclusion and systemic exclusion, diasporic communities.

The influx of nation-states around the world has not led to enduring global silos and the maintenance of 'national integrity' as once imagined by our ancestors, instead with technological advancement, the state has become both more powerful and more obsolete in the lives of citizens (but that is an argument for later in the book). Tololyan (1991, P. 5) determines that the forcefulness of diasporic communities in mobilizing and representing themselves as transnational organizations (with a collective identity) compels the nation-state to "confront the extent to which their boundaries are porous and their ostensible homogeneity a multicultural heterogeneity." Vertovec notes, "Diasporas play an increasingly significant part in the development of nation-building in poor countries and in ones which have undergone major transformation, such as Eastern European and former Soviet states", which he argues is related to access to resources and economic stability (2005). Garding (2013, P. 4) highlights the creation of numerous diaspora that occurred in Eastern Europe, she notes, "Nowhere did the diaspora conundrum appear as abruptly and near-uniformly as it did in Eastern Europe and Eurasia after 1989. Centuries of migration and frequently redrawn state borders meant that most states could claim to be the ethnic homeland of overseas diaspora populations, as well as to pockets of ethnic kin scattered in adjacent states." This intense and rapid dispersal of people blurred the traditional conception of diaspora as related to a singular national identity or ethnic group. Kalra, Kalhon, and Hutynuk make a critical argument in distinguishing diaspora from ethnicity in analysis, *ethnicity reinstates the nation-state as the legitimate social sphere in which boundaries are made ... Policies of nation-states play a dialectical role in the creation and maintenance of ethnic groups. It is here that diaspora can be seen as almost a contradictory force to ethnicity, as it draws attention away from the single nation-states and towards a potential multiplicity of nation-states or regions within states. (2005, P. 17)*

Diasporic populations blur the definitions and identification of citizenship. As stated, the concept of citizenship has evolved yet T.H. Marshall's standard three elements (which have been adopted and adapted by numerous theorists) of citizenship have remained essential to definitions: civil, political, and social rights. Civil rights include protecting rights that are necessary to the liberty of a person, such as free speech, free exercise of faith, and the right to own property. The political rights are most important to this author and include the right to participate in one's governance (e.g.: to vote) and to be included in the political process. As Somers argues in relation to Arendt's discussion of Jewish statelessness, "it is not freedom and autonomy from all social and political entities that liberate us to be rights-bearers. Instead, it is embeddedness, political membership, and social inclusion that are necessary to have any rights at all, especially the human right to life itself" (2008, P. 7). Elassi asserts,

*Although statelessness is a product of modernity and the nation-state, the stateless people are denied a modern political identity, which is often equated with a national identity. This is not only a structural injury but also an issue that haunts the stateless in their everyday lives, when the stateless people do not identify with the sovereign identity within which they are forcefully subsumed. (2015, P. 19)*

Finally, the social element focuses on economic security, a shared social heritage (inclusion in the society), and the right to progress within the society (Marshall, 1950, P. 10-11). While these three concepts of citizenship may seem rudimentary, they are still considered to be the base rights that a citizen can expect to be protected by a state to which they belong. Yet Vertovec (2005) reiterates, "Today, national/ethnic identification, political community, and place of residence do not automatically fit together neatly". As the discussion of diasporic politics unfolds in the following chapters, the three elements presented here will become more nuanced to the reader and provide for an updated way of considering citizenship in the future.

Somers goes onto define citizenship as the "right to have rights – not any single civil, juridical, or even social right, but the primary right of recognition, inclusion, and membership in both political and civil society" (2008, P. 25). She provides for a distinction between the formal rights that are key to Marshall's conception of citizenship, and the informal (or societal) right of being, or personhood. As discussed in Stacey (2018), the modern iteration of nationalism and nationalist politics taking over the international community has led to a dehumanization of the Other (whether that is Latinos, Muslims, women, or another marginalized group) which has provided for dangerous (and discriminatory) politics in countries including the United States, which have impacted (and jeopardized) the rights of citizens and non-citizens alike. Kalra, Kalhon, and Hutynuk (2005, P. 29) assert that the "deformation of the nation has implied both defensive, xenophobic posturing as well as progressive trans-ethnic and transnational alliances", noting the rise of right-wing, neo-Nazi, white supremacist associated groups in Europe and North America while simultaneously racialized groups become defensive and existential regarding their inclusion/belonging in the country. A salient example of how this nationalism is putting citizens at risk is the American response to recent hurricanes in the Commonwealth of Puerto Rico. Citizenship is often racialized, according to Hua (2011) and can in these events "fail to provide liberty, equality and security to certain racialized individuals" (P. 48).

The woeful conditions in Puerto Rico and the plight of American citizens living there should not be ignored, but because the people have been characterized differently than mainland Americans, the federal government's response to the concurrent natural disasters of 2017 has largely been underwhelming. Although the economically and geographically underprivileged population of Puerto Rico does possess American citizenship status, they were thought of as different and lesser than other members of the American society. Ho emphasizes, "Because of the new cultural racism, everyday commonsense racism, structural racism and scientific racism along with sexism and homophobia, many people of color, women, and non-heterosexuals in Euro-America feel a deep-seated sense of unbelonging, whether it is social, political, economical, cultural, or psychological" (2011, P. 50). Axel (2002, P. 246) notes that the conceptualization of the nation (often as the *best* or *unique*) is key to nationalism, which allows for the "possibility that any citizen may be a potential foe of the nation, the threat of cultural difference is not a problem of an alien element, a parasitic *other people*."

Hybridity, or the mixing of diasporic and host cultures/societies has been used theoretically as a justification for the Othering that is increasingly more common in the current (inter)transnational community. Kalra, Kalhon, and Hutynk (2005, P. 128) note that in this transnational world of terrorism, "Those 'others' who stand 'with' the USA, those who sign on as the safe 'communities of diaspora', distancing themselves from 'Muslims' and others who might look like them, are displayed as examples that serve to illustrate the compact where everyone can be brought into the modern ecumene of democracy", while at the same time giving warning to those diasporic communities who dare to engage in dissent or protest. The *us* versus *them* mentality was promulgated at the outset of the War on Terror by former President George W. Bush, and has become much more visible with the solidification of the Trump 'travel ban' in June 2018. Diasporic (or Other) communities in the United States have become suspect since the attacks on September 11, 2001, particularly within the Muslim-American community, which has led to a disintegration of tenuous lines that separated the social spheres and an increase in vandalism, violence, and the outright rejection of refugees (on the part of the government). In the face of transnational terrorism, an inward political turn toward nationalism, protecting of state sovereignty, defending the borders, and a strict rejection of the Other (whether that is a legitimate Other – citizen with varied ethnic composition; or illegitimate – non-citizens with varied ethnic composition living within a host country), no matter what the diasporic community has done to develop the state or society. As Demmers (2002, P. 93) aptly notes, "Contemporary nationalist struggles are largely counter-nationalistic: identity groups resist assimilation into the nation-state. In fact, every nationalist attempt to create a nation or a people at the same time creates national minorities, and potential new nationalisms." There is a counterintuitive nature to contemporary Western nationalism that establishes and reinforces diasporic and Other communities and their increased participation in the political (and civil) society, which is predominately what these nationalists are seeking to limit or eliminate altogether.

States have traditionally conceived of diaspora politics as international policy as opposed to considering the diasporic community within national borders to be a domestic policy area, where the state has considerable control (Delano and Gamlen, 2014). State-diaspora relations are important for political scientists when analyzing concepts such as place of origin, citizenship, national identity, and the policies put in place by the host country that may hinder or support a diasporic community. Garding (2013, P. 8) uses the term diasporic political incorporation policies to describe formal measures proposed or used by the State to facilitate or impede the diasporic community's membership, participation, and representation in the homeland [and host country] political community.

The 'travel ban' instituted by President Donald Trump in 2017 is an illuminating example of systematic Othering of an entire religion, and may have grave implications on the American image, politics, and society. The first iteration of the ban was signed into law via an executive order in January 2017 (January 27, to be exact), just days after the inauguration was complete, and sought to restrict (temporarily) travel into the U.S. from seven, predominately Muslim countries. Upon hearing the news, protestors and activists flooded American airports from coast-to-coast in opposition to the order, a federal judge from Seattle put the order on hold nationwide just a week after its implementation, on February 3. The second iteration of the Trump travel ban attempts to clean up the questionable (constitutionally) language regarding religion, but went farther than the first as well (Finnegan, 2017). The ban was signed on March 6, 2017 and removed Iraq from the list of seven countries from which travel is restricted, leaving six countries. The order also cleared up administrative chaos that was initiated by the first order in specifying that any person with a legal valid visa or legal permanent residents was exempted from the order (there were several stories in which military members or science fair teams were stopped from entering the country even though they were either visa holders or legal residents). The second order was challenged by Hawaii, arguing that the second order did not do enough to clarify that it was not a Muslim ban, as the president had discussed while a candidate for office in 2016. The order was again put on stay on March 15, and blocked altogether on May 25, when the Fourth Circuit Court voted 10-3 to stop major provisions of the travel ban from being implemented but did allow Trump's 120-day ban on refugees to remain intact.

After a summer of legal battles over the constitutionality, intent, and implementation of the second travel ban, on September 24, just as the second travel ban was set to expire, the Trump administration issued what amounted to the third iteration of its travel ban. This third ban barred travel from seven countries; Iran, Syria, Somalia, and Libya which were all part of the original travel ban, and adding Chad, Venezuela, and North Korea due to domestic political instability. The new ban established a criteria-based system, which means that the U.S. could add or remove countries from the ban as new conditions are evaluated. However, one day before the new restrictions were set to be implemented a district court judge in Hawaii issued a temporary restraining order, arguing that the new ban discriminates on the basis of nationality. After this set back, the Trump administration decided in October

2017 that it would just wait for the Supreme Court to rule on the constitutionality of the travel ban language instead of fighting constantly with district courts. In December 2017, Trump won a mild victory with the Supreme Court's decision to overrule a lower court and allow the third iteration of the ban to go into effect, which becomes a good omen among legal scholars as to how the Court will ultimately rule on the ban (Phillips, 2018).

In June 2018, the Supreme Court in a 5-4 decision came down on the side of the Trump administration and the executive branch's ability to unilaterally decide travel restrictions in the name of national security. The brief summarization of the Trump travel ban saga should lead to an understanding of how modern diasporic communities are created, and more importantly how they mobilize. The Othering of national origins, but more obviously, a religion should arguably lead to increased diasporic engagement with host country politics. Trump and his brand of nationalism (and nationalist policies) are having an adverse effect on the administration itself (and their loyalists), by singling out ethnic and religious communities for better or worse treatment leaves a sour taste in the mouths of those who ascribe to that religion or were born into that ethnic community and makes diasporic protest more likely in the host country. It becomes difficult in a country such as the United States, which has long been the harbinger of democracy and a nation of diversity, to reinstitute and re-litigate the politics of the Other as well as policies that exalt some over others in a society. There are native-born Muslims in the U.S., there are Iranian-Americans, or Syrian-Americans who are now having to choose between their place of origin and human (civil) rights.

Refugees are an important factor in contemporary diaspora studies. According to the United Nations 2017 International Migration Report, there were an estimated 25.9 million refugees and asylum-seekers around the world in 2016 (an effective year for international coalition forces fighting the Islamic State). As a result of the fight against terrorism, namely the Islamic State, an estimated 3.1 million of those refugees fled and are being housed in Turkey; 2.9 million in Jordan; 2.2 million in the State of Palestine; 1.6 million in Lebanon; and 1.4 million in Pakistan. As noted the influx of contemporary refugee/asylum-seekers does tend to revolve around the West's ongoing presence in Middle East affairs, yet there is a group of migrants that are refugees not of a political or military conflict, but of globalization. This argument was much more prevalent in the late 1990s and early-to-mid 2000s, yet with sanctions on Russia, North Korea, China (in relation to North Korea), and a potential to reinstate the massive sanctions on Iran, there is still a need to acknowledge the economic refugee. As Sivanandan asserts,

*Even genuine refugees and asylum-seekers are being sent back to the countries they have escaped from on the grounds that they are economic and not political refugees, which overlooks the fact that it is the authoritarian regimes maintained by western governments, in Third World countries, on behalf of transnational companies, that throw up refugees on western shores. It is your economics that makes our politics that makes us refugees in your countries. (1997)*

The concept that this work grapples with is diasporic politics and how people/nations self-determine (or are able to integrate into a new nation-state's culture and politics, or how a new nation-state is born in this tumultuous global political environment). According to Charusheela (2007, P. 280), "Diaspora is a term that situates analyses of subject formation and social experience in a transnational context. It thus draws attention to the cross-border transactions that shape social, psychic, and experiential subjects." Transnationalism as discussed throughout this work as Ong (2003) describes, "...to describe the processes of disembbeding from a set of localized relations in the homeland nation and re-embedding in new overlapping networks that cut across borders" (P. 87). In the spirit of this conception of diaspora, this work probes questions such as, how does one who immigrates become a citizen and acknowledged quantity in the host state beyond the political and legal processes is a focus of the women's movement case study; and the other focuses on the plight of diasporic communities around the world in attempting to gain international attention for their self-determination causes.

Technological advancements (e.g.: the internet, social media platforms, cellphones) have exacerbated the problem for nation-states attempting to craft and solidify what citizenship means in the 21st century. The conceptualization, much less, the acceptance of any one place as *home* or ideals (or qualifications for citizenship) has become complicated in the post-globalization era (or the globalized world). Cho (2007, P. 468) notes, "Citizenship in the form granted by the nation-state cannot fully encompass the multiple modes of belonging that are actually practiced". There are various forms of citizenship that extend beyond the formal recognition of a person or peoples by the state apparatus, including cultural and sentimental, which are often promulgated by those digital technologies that dominate our collective existence in the modern day. The transnational nature of movement in the digital age of peoples, capital, resources, and information mean that "the stranger is always in proximity" or that the Other is closer to our home than previously thought (Ahmed, 2000, P. 13). Simmel (1971) describes the *stranger* as a trader that "lives within a particular community but always attendant to an elsewhere" (P. 144), for Simmel, the stranger occupies many spaces simultaneously, yet belongs in none of them. This is a brilliant metaphor for diaspora, and what it means to both build a home yet not feel at home there. There is seemingly a detachment from place that exists in contemporary diaspora (as conveyed largely via the interviews in Chapter Four) that takes the spotlight off of the nation-state/territorial conceptions of diasporic consciousness or identity. Kalra, Kalhon, and Hutynuk (2005, P. 32) argue, "Deterritorialization implies staking identity outside originary claims to land. These non-territorial claims may still be about nationality, but they cannot make the argument that this sense of nationality is derived from the land."

Transnationalism describes a broader set of processes that is able to divorce the human or group dynamics that are entrenched in diaspora. Transnationalism, according to Vertovec (1999, P. 447) concerns "the multiple ties and interactions linking people or institutions across the borders of the nation-states" and "describes forces that cross or work across the nation's boundaries but do not necessarily disrupt the workings of the nation-state as executive committee" (Kalra, Kalhon, and Hutynuk, 2005, P. 34). Ang (2003, P. 3) summarizes how the nation-state is situated in the transnational environment, arguing, "...The nation-state is cast as the limiting, homogenizing, assimilating power structure, which is now, finally, being deconstructed from within by those groups who used to be marginalized within its borders but are now bursting out of them through their diasporic transnational connections."

Wimmer and Glick Schiller (2002) assert that transnationalism as an academic concept transcended "methodological nationalism", or the inclination of research to privilege the nation-state as the essential component of sociological analysis (P. 301). Transnationalism blurs the relationship between the state and diaspora, as it involves varied conceptions of citizenship and belonging in the contemporary international community that is interconnected in numerous ways. Transnational forms of citizenship look beyond geographic designations of boundary and note that citizenship exists beyond the state (in the same manner as national identity).

Ahmed goes onto note that in a digital, transnational world,

*Home is here, not a particular place that one simply inhabits, but more than one place; there are too many homes to allow place to secure the roots or routes of one's journey between homes provide the subject with the contours of a space of belonging, but a space that expresses the very logic of an interval, the passing through of the subject between apparently fixed moments of departure and arrival. (2000, P. 77)*

Literature on diaspora has expanded from merely the territorial and political, to more psychological (and affective) aspects of diaspora, and what it means to not have a home *or* the perception that your homeland is not an inclusive place. Charusheela notes that "narratives of diaspora tell of how one came to move across varied types of boundaries, of how one grew up as a stranger at home, of the histories through which one came to occupy this place between two nations, and of how one then navigates experience between two nations, two communities" (2007, P. 285). This work will look at both the political (thus territorial) concepts associated with diaspora politics in relation to Kurdish self-determination as well as expand on the political psychology of diaspora politics in relation to the women's movements going on around the world. In both dissections of contemporary diaspora politics, the author will use historical institutionalism to provide for greater context into the cases and peoples affected. This book is comparative and qualitative, using primary sources (e.g.: interviews with Middle Eastern women who immigrated to the U.S.) and secondary sources (news articles, journals, books, reports, etc.) to paint a clear picture of what is at stake for those 'strangers in a strange land' attempting to find themselves and a place to belong. The work will also touch upon the wider #metoo movement and the psychological (and often systemic social) displacement that many women feel in their homelands, or the diaspora at home.

## Diasporic Literature

Baumann (2000) asserts that diaspora entered the academic realm via African studies scholars in the 1960s in relation to the Jewish experience (dating back to biblical times), diaspora in a classical sense relates to forced migration, but as discussed, the term has evolved to include sentimental aspects. Yet it is less problematic for social scientists to discuss 'transnational' as opposed to 'diaspora' because of the following selected (often stringent) set of criteria that theorists' maintain defines diaspora, with particular emphasis on the idea of 'place of origin' and the concept of home (imagined or actual). Karla, Kalhon, and Hutynuk (2005) that although there has been a hybridity added to the connotation of diaspora, yet "a turn away from institutional structures does not necessarily mean a lack of concern with politics. Certain diasporic formations can sit easily in the political culture of a nation-state while others do not" (P. 15). Again, here it is worth reiterating, this author is presenting the concept of diaspora in both the physical/territorial form, as well as the oft-critiqued psychological/sentimental form because it does appear that both forms are salient in contemporary international politics.

Cohen (1997) articulates four phases of diaspora studies, which provides a helpful map to introducing diaspora literature to new readers as well as the application of theory to contemporary case studies. Cohen argues that the study of diaspora has evolved through four stages that are articulated/distinguished by temporal as well as ideological developments in thinking about what it means to be stateless, and more recently, toward more sentimental aspects of diaspora. Cohen expresses the four phases starting with the classical use of diaspora as "mainly confined to the study of the Jewish experience", which was extended due to migration of various other populations in the mid-to-late 20$^{th}$ century (Cohen notes the use of the term to describe African, Armenian, and Irish diffusion).

The second phase, which Cohen notes begins in the 1980s to the emergence of the third phase in the mid-1990s, diaspora as a concept extended to "different categories of people – expatriates, expellees, political refugees, alien residents, immigrants, and ethnic and racial minorities" who both applied the label to themselves and had it thrust upon them by nationals (Cohen, 2008, P. 1). As stated, the third phase according to Cohen began in the mid-1990s, diasporic theorists became influenced by postmodernism and social constructivism and began to deconstruct "two of the major building blocks previously delimiting and demarcating the diasporic idea, namely 'homeland' and 'ethnic/religious community'" (Cohen, 2008, P. 1-2). This is further discussed in the gender diaspora chapter, but is worth noting that the third phase coincides with the proliferation of digital technologies in the mid-1990s and would have arguably been the start of transnational identity construction, as the third phase argued that "identities have become deterritorialized and constructed and deconstructed in a flexible and situational way" (Cohen, 2008, P. 2).

Anthias finds the construction of transnational identities advantageous, not simply for diaspora studies, but in understanding each other, noting "the perception of diaspora as breaking 'the ethnic spectacles' with which the world was previously viewed, may vastly underestimate the continuing attachment to the idea of ethnic and therefore particularist bonds, to a new reconstructed form of ethnic absolutism" (1998, P. 567). Finally, Cohen argues by the 21$^{st}$ century the concept of diaspora has undergone a "phase of consolidation [that] is marked by a modified reaffirmation of the diasporic idea, including its core elements, common features and ideal types (which include ideas of home).

Cohen's third and fourth phases, where the concept of diaspora is expanded, is where this work situates itself among diaspora literature/theory. Although the third phase Cohen argument is adapted a bit by recognizing that "diaspora was chic" to instead articulate an understanding that development of the characterization of what diaspora means needed to be more inclusive (2008, P. 8). Cohen's argument that by eliminating or blurring the essential elements of defining diasporic populations allows for anyone to claim diaspora (which he labels "a craze"), according Brubaker (2005, P.), "as the term has proliferated its meaning has been stretched to accommodate the various intellectual, cultural and political agendas in the service of which it has been enlisted. This has resulted in what one might call a 'diaspora' diaspora – a dispersion of the meaning of the term in semantic, conceptual and disciplinary space." However, this author argues that it is worth considering that there are varying elements of defining (or characterizing) diaspora that require consideration on an analytical level (such as queer or gender diaspora).

Psychological elements of diaspora challenge the basic tenant of diaspora studies regarding the concept of *home*. Instead of a territorial concept complete with boundaries/borders, laws, languages, cultures, etc., home becomes a more sentimental concept, which has not always pleased the more quantitative social scientists. This is not to completely discredit the role the nation-state plays in diasporic politics of particular groups, e.g. the Kurds, who are (through their ethnic/religious identity) attempting to establish their own homeland (country), which highlights the importance of considering ethnonational, cultural, and political ties when examining various diasporas. Kalra, Kalhon, and Hutynuk (2005, P. 22) note "...the central contradiction of all mobilizations for statehood that gain much of their force from diasporas; they are always open to the criticism that it is the diaspora's concerns about identity which are being played out, often violently, in the homeland." Thus although the overall influence of the nation-state on diaspora and/or identity has been blurred in the digital age, it does still play a major role in the identification of particular diasporic communities across the world. As Sayyid notes,

*The diaspora is not the other of the nation simply because it is constructed from the antithetical elements of nation, it is, rather, an anti-nation since it interrupts the closure of nation. The existence of a diaspora prevents the closure of the nation, since a diaspora is by definition located within another nation. (2000, P. 42)*

During the so-called consolidation phase of diaspora studies (Cohen, 1997), where the concepts of home and belonging became more theoretical (or psychologically linked), Tololyan (1991) argued that attachment to a place was still crucial to the field, which reiterated the sentiment previously expressed by Armstrong (1976, P. 393), arguing, "Clearly, a diaspora is something more than, say, a collection of persons distinguished by some secondary characteristic such as, for example, all persons with Scottish names in Wisconsin...the mobilized diaspora has often constituted for centuries a separate society or quasi-society in a larger polity". Boundaries and borders have shaped the international community since Westphalia, but as has been argued by numerous theorists, (e.g., Tilly, 2011; Castells 1996, 2001, 2010, etc.) the influx of digital technologies has ushered in a transnational global order that provides greater opportunity for diasporic populations to communicate and foment dissent while potentially not being in proximity of each other or the homeland (real or imagined). Tololyan states,

*Diasporists shaped by globalizing discourse describe genuine erosions of the link between a bounded place and a people, diagnose it as irresistible, and quickly affirm its contribution to a pluralistic, multicultural, hybrid world of which they approve. Diasporists like myself, who want to argue that attachment to place was indispensable to diasporic life and thought until very recently, and that despite its erosion it remains important today, must tread carefully in order to avoid the charge that we are either imitating discredited nationalist rhetoric about the link between land, people, and culture, or that we remain naïve about the global spaces that have opened in the past several decades. (1991, P. 7)*

Kalra, Kalhon, and Hutynuk (2005, P. 17) assert "if there is any single theme that emerges from a study of diaspora, it is that of its multi-locational qualities, or the interaction between homes and abroads which cannot be reduced to one place or another", which is a prescient state regarding the impending social media revolution that would provide a much more trans-and-international network (Twitter would become publicly accessible in July 2006; Facebook was accessible to a limited grouping in 2004, and became publicly accessible to anyone with an email address in September 2006). The authors highlight "the developing interconnectivity across international borders has meant that those with access are now able, to various extents, to maintain connections, deepen relationships and broaden networks with lesser investment in terms of time, cost and effort" (2005, P. 19). This interconnectedness provides diasporic populations with stronger connections and new ways (and tools) to mobilize people and resources that transcend nation-state boundaries, including in social movement tactics and ideology (see Stacey, 2018). According to Ragazzi and Balalovska,

*The characteristic of this new form of post-territorial citizenship is to abandon the territorial referent as the main criterion for inclusion and exclusion from citizenship, focusing instead on ethno-cultural markers of identity, irrespective of the place of residence...It advocates inclusion and attribution of equal rights and privileges to ethnic groups or "communities" cohabiting on the same territorial unit. (2011, P. 4)*

In accordance with the evolution of the concept (and characterization) of diaspora, Vertovec (1998) provides three categorizations of diaspora: 1) diaspora as a social form; 2) diaspora as a type of consciousness; and 3) diaspora as a mode of cultural production. As a social form (which is crucial to mobilization of diasporic populations), there are three aspects Vertovec characterizes as essential, including social relationships that are "related to common origins and migration routes" as well as potential transference of political loyalty from the homeland to the state of resettlement (1999, P.). This work also places emphasis on Vertovec's second definition of diaspora in relation to consciousness, which relates to the psychological and sentimental aspects of diasporic populations and the act of resettling in a new land. Karim argues,

*Diasporas (re)create home by instilling such resonance into the spaces: they do it with their languages, customs, art forms, arrangement of objects and ideas. Their media, especially the electronic, reterritorialize the diaspora through the resonance of electromagnetic frequencies. However, the milieus that diasporas seek to create are not bounded by the borders of nation-states – their rhythms resonate transnationally to mark out the non-terrestrial spaces that stretch out inter-continentally. (2007, P. 273)*

As Kalra, Kalhon, and Hutynuk (2005) argue, there is a "hybridity" that describes contemporary diasporic populations and the blending of cultures in the host society, not akin to assimilation but more an integration of societies, cultures, languages, etc., creating the modern cosmopolitan state. This process arguably began with globalization and the proliferation of information across nations, which includes recipes, social movement tactics, political consciousness, and much more. Chambers (1996) argues that hybridity (in relation to diaspora) is most closely associated with a melding of cultures (both the culture of origin and the newly adopted host country) where the diasporic member is navigating tradition as well as adapting to the host country, this reconfiguration is, for Chambers, the development of hybrid identities. As will be discussed in Chapter Four, the majority of the interviewees expressed a sense of hybridity that seemed to be necessary to maintain. It is important to note here that this author is uncertain about the concept of cultural or national purity (as opposed to the concept of hybridity). It seems increasingly unlikely in the contemporary international community that any nation is pure in any sense of the word, but certainly not ethnically, religiously, culturally, etc. (with the exception, perhaps, of North Korea). As Gilroy argues, "Whether the process of mixture is presented as fatal or redemptive, we must be prepared to give up the illusion that cultural and ethnic purity has ever existed, let alone provided a foundation for civil society" (2000, P. 250).

Hybridity remains an important concept for current analysis of diaspora as it relates to the psychological and cultural obligations that are necessary for resettlement in a new land (or as it relates to the case study on gender diaspora). While the notion of hybridity does beg questions of gentrification, assimilation, acculturation, and a replacement of diaspora identity – it is hybridity that made the United States the great 'melting pot' that has been celebrated for its diversity and lack of true national identity (meaning, there is no one right way to *be* an American, to *look* American, to *speak* American). Papastergiadis (2000) notes that while hybridity has encouraged the development of a global identity (as opposed to national), the concept does have a debilitating power to blur the differences that hybridity (and more certainly, diaspora) should promote. Werbner (2002, P. 121) asserts, "... diasporas are not simply aesthetic communities; nor are they merely reflections of the displaced or hybrid consciousness of individual diasporic subjects: on the contrary, diasporas are usually highly politicized social formations." Felski (1997) promotes the necessity of considering contemporary diasporas and diasporic politics through the lens of hybridity. Felski argues,

*Metaphors of hybridity and the like not only recognize differences within the subject, fracturing and complicating holistic notions of identity, but also address connections between subjects by recognizing affiliations cross-pollinations, echoes and repetitions, thereby unseating difference from a position of absolute privilege. Instead of endorsing a drift towards ever-greater atomization of identity, such metaphors allow us to conceive of multiple, interconnecting axes of affiliation and differentiation. (1997, P. 12)*

Kalra, Kalhon, and Hutynuk (2005) conclude, "Diaspora and hybridity recognize the disruption of privilege, but do not offer the means to displace it, and the massive military-legalistic forces that ensure its continuity", thus providing for more inclusion and analysis of diaspora politics and circumstances, yet the authors clearly warn against mistakenly believing that the nation-state apparatus is rendered wholly obsolete. The privilege and influence of the state is still quite apparent in decisions such as the travel ban discussed previously, which can have a direct impact on not just the diasporic community within the host nation, but beyond. Hybridity then, involves interactions, intersections, and collective engagements, "it necessarily implies a softening of the boundaries between *peoples*: the encounters between them are as constitutive of who they are as the proceedings within" (Ang, 2003, P. 6).

The following chapter examines contemporary and new social movement literature to provide a basic understanding of mobilization and other theories that are essential to the fomenting of a collective identity into an active community (whether diasporic or social movement-oriented). The chapter also introduces theories on networked or digital social movements and the utilization of new (available) technologies by social movement and diasporic organizations. The theories emphasized in Chapter Two include the life cycle of social problems thesis by Herbert Blumer (1971) and Martin Sökefeld's (2006) theory of diasporic mobilization, which is largely based on prominent social movement theorists such as Charles Tilly.

## REFERENCES

Ahmed, S. (2000). *Strange Encounters: Embodied Others in Post-Coloniality*. London: Routledge.

Ang, I. (2003). Together-in-difference: Beyond Diaspora, into Hybridity. *Asian Studies Review*, *27*(2), 141–154. doi:10.1080/10357820308713372

Anthias, F. (1998). Evaluating Diaspora: Beyond Ethnicity? *Sociology*, *32*(3), 557–580.

Anzaldua, G. (1987). *Borderlands/La Frontera: The New Mestiza*. Aunt Lute Books.

Armstrong, J. (1976). Mobilized and proletarian diasporas. *The American Political Science Review*, *70*(2), 393–408. doi:10.2307/1959646

Axel, B. (2002). National Interruption: Diaspora Theory and Multiculturalism in the UK. *Cultural Dynamics*, *14*(3), 235–256. doi:10.1177/09213740020140030101

Baumann, M. (2000). Diaspora: Genealogies of semantics and transcultural comparison. *Numen*, *47*(3), 313–337. doi:10.1163/156852700511577

Blumer, H. (1971). Social Problems as Collective Behavior. *Social Problems*, *18*(Winter), 298–306. doi:10.2307/799797

Brubaker, R. (2005). The 'diaspora' diaspora. *Ethnic and Racial Studies*, *28*(1), 1–19. doi:10.1080/0141987042000289997

Chambers, I. (1996). Signs of Silence, Lines of Listening. In I. Chambers & L. Curtis (Eds.), *The Post-Colonial Question* (pp. 47–62). London: Routledge. doi:10.4324/9780203297865

Charusheela, S. (2007). The Diaspora at Home. *Cultural Dynamics*, *19*(2/3), 279–300. doi:10.1177/0921374007080295

Cho, L. (2007). The Turn to Diaspora. *Topia*, *17*, 11–30. doi:10.3138/topia.17.11

Cohen, R. (1997/2008). *Global Diasporas: An Introduction*. London: University College London Press. doi:10.4324/9780203228920

Délano, A., & Gamlen, A. (2014). Comparing and Theorizing State–diaspora Relations. *Political Geography*, *41*, 43–53. doi:10.1016/j.polgeo.2014.05.005

Demmers, J. (2002). Diaspora and Conflict: Locality, Long-Distance Nationalism, and Delocalization of Conflict Dynamics. *The Public*, *9*(1), 85–96.

Elassi, B. (2015). *Narratives of Statelessness and Political Belonging Among Kurdish Diasporas in Sweden and the UK*. International Migration Institute, Working Paper 114, Oxford University.

Felski, R. (1997). The doxa of difference. *Signs (Chicago, Ill.)*, *23*(1), 1–22. doi:10.1086/495231

Finnegan, C. (2017). A Timeline of Trump's Battle with the Courts to Keep his Travel Ban Alive. *ABC News*. Accessed from: https://abcnews.go.com/Politics/timeline-trumps-battle-courts-travel-ban-alive/story?id=50559798

Ganguly, K. (1992). Migrant Identities: Personal Memory and the Construction of Self-hood. *Cultural Studies*, *6*(1), 27–50. doi:10.1080/09502389200490021

Garding, S. E. (2013). *Courting the nation abroad: Diaspora political incorporation policies after communism* (Order No. 3720508). Available from Ethnic NewsWatch; ProQuest Dissertations & Theses Global. (1726022976)

Gilroy, P. (2000). *Between Camps*. London: Allen Lane.

Ho, E. L.-E. (2011). Claiming the Diaspora: Elite Mobility, Sending State Strategies and the Spatialities of citizenship. *Progress in Human Geography*, *35*(6), 757–772. doi:10.1177/0309132511401463

Hua, A. (2011). Homing Desire, Cultural Citizenship, and Diasporic Imaginings. *Journal of International Women's Studies*, *12*(4), 45–56.

Kalra, V., Kalhon, R., & Hutynuk. (2005). *Diaspora and Hybridity*. London: Sage Publications.

Karim, K. (Ed.). (2002). *The Media of Diaspora*. London: Routledge.

Karim, K. (2007). Nation and diaspora: Rethinking multiculturalism in a transnational context. *International Journal of Media & Cultural Politics*, *2*(3), 267–282. doi:10.1386/macp.2.3.267_1

Marshall, T. H. (1950). *Citizenship and Social Class: And Other Essays*. Cambridge, UK: Cambridge University Press.

Nititham, D. S. (2008). Locating the self in diaspora space. T*ranslocations: The Irish Migration. Race and Social Transformation Review*, *3*(1), 1–17.

Ong, A. (2003). *Flexible Citizenship: The Cultural Logics of Transnationality*. Durham, NC: Duke University Press.

Papastergiadis, N. (2000). *The Turbulence of Migration: Globalization, Deterritorialization and Hybridity*. Cambridge, UK: Polity Press.

Phillips, A. (2018). Analysis: A Brief Rundown of the Long Legal History of Trump's Travel Ban. *Washington Post.* Accessed from: https://www.washingtonpost.com/news/the-fix/wp/2018/06/26/a-brief-rundown-of-the-long-legal-history-of-trumps-travel-ban/?utm_term=.404a217c7882

Ragazzi, F., & Balalovska, K. (2011). *Diaspora Politics and Post-Territorial Citizenship in Croatia, Serbia and Macedonia.* European Research Council, Working Paper, The University of Edinburgh.

Sayyid, S. (2000). Beyond Westphalia: Nations and Diasporas – the Case of the Muslim *Umma*. In B. Hesse (Ed.), *Un/Settled Multiculturalisms: Diasporas, Entanglements, Transruptions*. London: Zed Books.

Simmel, G. (1971). The Stranger. In *On Individuality and Social Forms*. Chicago: Univ. of Chicago Press.

Sivanandan, A. (1997). *On Fortress Europe (Speech).* Accessed from: www.irr.org.uk/sound/people/siva.ram

Sökefeld, M. (2006). Mobilizing in transnational space: A social movement approach to the formation of diaspora. *Global Networks*, *6*(3), 265–284. doi:10.1111/j.1471-0374.2006.00144.x

Somers, M. R. (2008). *Genealogies of Citizenship. Markets, Statelessness, and the Right to Have Rights*. Cambridge, UK: Cambridge University Press.

Stacey, E. (2017). *Combatting Internet-Enabled Terrorism: Emerging Research and Opportunities*. IGI Global. doi:10.4018/978-1-5225-2190-7

Stacey, E. (2018). *Nationalism, Social Movements, and Activism: Emerging Research and Opportunities*. IGI Global. doi:10.4018/978-1-5225-5433-2

Tölölyan, K. (1991). The nation-state and its others: In lieu of a preface. *Diaspora*, *1*(1), 3–7. doi:10.1353/dsp.1991.0008

United Nations. (2017). *International Migration Report*. Retrieved from http://www.un.org/en/development/desa/population/migration/publications/migrationreport/docs/MigrationReport2017_Highlights.pdf

Vertovec, S. (1998). Three meanings of "diaspora", exemplified among South Asian religions. *Diaspora*, *6*(3), 277–300. doi:10.1353/dsp.1997.0010

Vertovec, S. (1999). Conceiving and researching transnationalism. *Ethnic and Racial Studies*, *22*(2), 447–462. doi:10.1080/014198799329558

Werbner, P. (2002). The place which is diaspora: Citizenship, religion and gender in the making of chaordic transnationalism. *Journal of Ethnic and Migration Studies*, *28*(1), 119–134. doi:10.1080/13691830120103967

Wimmer, A., & Glick Schiller, N. (2002). Methodological nationalism and beyond: Nation-state building, migration and the social sciences. *Global Networks*, *2*(4), 301–334. doi:10.1111/1471-0374.00043

# Chapter 2
# New (and Networked) Social Movement Literature


## ABSTRACT

*This chapter provides a summary of new social movement literature, with a particular focus on the phases that social movements progress through as well as the tools (namely digital) that are being used to establish diaspora (as well as social movement) networks across the international community and provide for mobilization. The chapter particularly focuses on the theories of Herbert Blumer (Life Cycle of Social Problems) and Martin Sökefeld, who writes about mobilization of various diasporic communities using social movement theory. The chapter also focuses on identity theories and the importance of developing of collective identities for effective mobilization of movement communities (diasporic and social movement).*


## INTRODUCTION

Hua (2011) re-introduces the concept of "dissident citizenship" that was first proposed by Sparks (1997) to note the increasing phenomenon of performing protest or dissident actions by a marginalized community to upset the political elite to make legitimate claims to egalitarian participation in the greater society. In the same manner as social movement organizations, dissident citizens use "alternative public spaces" and tactics such as protesting, demonstrations, speeches, and occupation of public spaces to make their argument for democratic inclusion. Often, these contemporary scenes of dissident citizen

DOI: 10.4018/978-1-5225-7757-7.ch002

Copyright © 2019, IGI Global. Copying or distributing in print or electronic forms without written permission of IGI Global is prohibited.

activism (such as the Palestinian peoples attempting to reach the border wall separating them from Israel proper to be met with sometimes fatal violence on the part of the Israeli government) spread awareness or publicizes the inequity and often, violent opposition that *non-citizens* (perceived or actual) experience around the world. These actions (and reactions by the State) can elevate the plight of certain groups to regional and international awareness, and can place pressure (internal, by lawful citizens and external, by international allies) on the political establishment inflicting the discriminatory policies to reform their thinking and treatment of the Other within their borders.

In considering social movements within or among diasporic communities, often these movements are fomenting the collective power of excluded, marginalized, or oppressed populations into dissent and calls for sociopolitical change (including frequent challenges to the existing power structure). Social justice movements, such as #metoo and Black Lives Matter (which would encompass diaspora movements for recognition/human rights) are distinguished by six characteristics according to Batliwala and Brown (2006): a base of participants that are mobilized and share mutual concerns; the existence of organizations (whether formal or informal); continuity over time; a clearly articulated and defined political agenda; collective actions (demonstrations, protests, rallies) in pursuit of the movement's goals; and the use of varied strategies and tactics. This chapter provides a brief overview of contemporary social movement and diaspora movement literature. The focus on theories of digital or networked social movements is important as well as analysis of the life cycle of social movements provides the reader with a detailed understanding as to how and why mobilization occurs.

This chapter particularly reasserts the importance of emotionality in connection with sociality in mobilization of contemporary movements that are aided by digital media and the internet. It is not enough to focus on the life cycle of a social movement without explaining the individual circumstances of each case study, which will be found in the Emergence section and the Mobilization (Coalescence) section that follows, and will place emphasis on communicative organization of participants and awareness among the community. This emphasis will be on multilateral media such as social media and argue that the often the new media feed from the bottom-up, content that comes directly from those on the ground, experiencing the movement firsthand. The multidirectional, multilateral media network allows for the presence of connected individuals as well as a protest network that brings together those individuals by emphasizing shared grievances. Both of the initial stages of social movements are crucial to the solidification of the movement as a formidable opponent to the status quo, and communication and the spread of ideology (goals, philosophy of the movement, the movement culture) through new media is fundamental. This is simply an infusion of digital technologies into the concepts of emergence and coalescence that Blumer (1971) and Sökefeld (2006) perceive as the first stages of movements.

## SÖKEFELD AND BLUMER: THEORIES ON THE PROGRESSION OF SOCIAL MOVEMENTS

In highlighting social movement theory and diaspora politics using Sökefeld (diaspora theorist) and Blumer (social movement theorist), this author thinks it prudent to begin with an explanation of Blumer's lesser-known thesis on the evolution of social problems (movements, for the purposes of this work). Herbert Blumer's stages of *social problems* are considered an important methodological framework from which this author analyzes the selected case studies. Blumer noted in 1971, the emergence of social problems (definition extended for this work to encompass social movements including protests, revolutions, etc.) and the lifecycle of these problems within a society. The five stages that social problems progress through are "emergence… legitimization or coalescence…mobilization…bureaucratization [and]…decline" (Blumer, 1971, P. 302-3).

1. **Emergence:** This stage includes the identification of a problem within a society, for Blumer, a social problem does not exist ***until*** and ***unless*** it is recognized as such by society. The emergence of social problems can vary in incubation periods to be recognized as an issue within society. Some problems are taken on immediately by a public as seen in the Icelandic Kitchenware movement, while others are largely ignored for greater peace and security for decades, only to be recognized as a problem at a political advantageous moment (political opportunity), as the world saw during the various Arab Spring movements, or more recently in the Black Lives Matter movement. Blumer contends that the media does not play a role until the legitimization process. This thesis contends that the processes of emergence and legitimation (coalescence) have been combined in the digital age. Awareness usually spawns an immediate emotional reaction from potential participants and regular citizens alike. The role of the media in contemporary movements is evident from the onset of organization.

2. **Legitimization or Coalescence:** Blumer (1955, 1969) notes that if a social problem is going to progress on its path, it must acquire social legitimacy. The social problem must garner enough attention and respectability to be discussed in the public sphere in order to facilitate mobilization and foster participation in the movement. Simply because a social problem is identified as serious and attracts attention does not mean that the issue will break into the public discourse. Thus, suggesting that social problems, though recognized in society, can be blocked from mainstream discourse (made taboo) by entities that wield more power than the people, for instance, the government or the broadcast media. This censorship (or blatant neglect) of social problems is much harder for governments and other major entities to commit in the digital age, which is contributing to the increased knowledge across the world and the subsequent reaction (including mobilization) by many groups.
3. **Mobilization:** At this stage, the social problem(s) have been identified and become a source of much discussion and controversy. Those in society who want to change or solve the problem gather like-minded individuals to facilitate a movement on behalf of the changes sought. These protestors are often met with battles against those in society who see no problem and want to continue the status quo. During mobilization, there is much "discussion, advocacy, evaluation, falsification, diversionary tactics and advancing of proposals tak[ing] place in the media of communication" (Blumer, 1971, P. 304). The progression of the movement to cure the social problem is dependent on the proper identification and framing of the social problem to the masses in order to create effective mobilization of supporters and participants.
4. **Bureaucratization:** This stage is questionable in new social movements. While many scholars will contend that it is necessary for a social movement to have institutionalized support at some organizational level as a determinant of success, this thesis and particularly, this chapter will show that bureaucratization or the incorporation of a social movement into an official apparatus of civil society is unnecessary to mobilize and sustain dissent. Movements in the digital age are creating institutions as they mobilize support and galvanize dissent. In long-term movements whose goals are regime change, bureaucratization or at least acknowledgement by some previously legitimized entity is necessary. For example, the Egyptian military defecting to support the mass protestors in both the 2011 and 2013 movements that led to the ousting of Mubarak and the first democratically elected president, Mohammad Morsi served as a

delegitimizing moment for the regime. There is also much speculation regarding the role of the Muslim Brotherhood in the movement that resulted in the removal of Mubarak, long-time Brotherhood adversary. During this stage, Blumer (1971, P. 305) describes a "formation of an official plan of action" and requires "new lines of action on the part of those involved in the social problem and those touched by the plan". Many social movements, particularly new social movements have gathered an idea about their plan of action well before a formal process or input from an organizational elite. Blumer (1971, P. 305) warns that "the administration and the operating personnel are prone to substitute their policies for the official policy underlying the plan [of action]," meaning that it is easy for the entity bureaucratizing the movement to supplement the agreed upon plan of action with their own intentions and moral prescriptions for solving the issue. Weber (1978) argues that bureaucratic organizations were structured to remove individualism and group dynamics in order to reinforce conformity of behavior and attitude. This stage is defined by formalization (Della Porta & Diani, 2006) and includes higher levels of organization and coalition-based strategies. Social movements that make it to this stage are no longer relying on mass demonstrations to garner attention but are reliant on administrative coordination and staff of social movement organizations or the bureaucratizing entity. Political power is arguably increased during this stage because the movement should have greater access to political elites, thus increasing their influence. Bureaucratization would include the efforts of diasporic organizations and groups that advocate for and on behalf of transnational diasporic communities, as defined in the Preface.

5. **Decline:** Miller (1999) notes four reasons for the decline of social movements, these are mainly organizational or strategic: "1) Repression; 2) Co-option; 3) Success; and 4) Failure".

Though Blumer's stages of social problems provides an elegant place from which to build, his concept of the progression of social problems does run into obvious theoretical pitfalls when applying to contemporary movements, those that are digital and post-digital. The following case studies illustrate contemporary social movements aided by the use of digital technologies. By dissecting the phases or stages that these contemporary movements progress through Blumer's framework, this thesis seeks to address commonalities and differences among new social movements under varying categories (protest and riots, regime change, sustained social justice movements) leading to a significant contribution to the study of collective action in the digital and post-digital age.

This work particularly reasserts the importance of emotionality in connection with sociality in mobilization of contemporary movements that are aided by digital media and the internet. It is not enough to focus on the life cycle of a social movement without explaining the individual circumstances of each case study, and will place emphasis on communicative organization of participants and awareness among the community. This emphasis will be on multilateral media such as social media and argue that the often the new media feed from the bottom-up, content that comes directly from those on the ground, experiencing the movement firsthand. The multidirectional, multilateral media network allows for the presence of connected individuals as well as a protest network that brings together those individuals by emphasizing shared grievances. Both of the initial stages of social movements are essential to the solidification of the movement as a formidable opponent to the status quo, and communication and the spread of ideology (goals, philosophy of the movement, the movement culture) through new media is fundamental. This is simply an infusion of digital technologies into the concepts of emergence and coalescence that Blumer saw as the first stages of movements.

Where Blumer diverges from the concepts of new social movement theory and the movements themselves is the idea of *bureaucratization* or *institutionalization*. The idea that movements still require the foundation of previous movements or the organizational structure of a non-governmental or civil organization that can 'administer' the movement effectively is counterintuitive to the nature of digital era social movements. Many new social movements are self-bureaucratizing and institutionalizing, which diverges entirely from Blumer and traditional theories of movements. This is true for contemporary movements such as Black Lives Matter, the organization and movement are self-bureaucratizing and eschewing traditional networks of political and social life in America, which are generally viewed as the vehicles to change. Numerous diasporic organizations are also involved in the bureaucratization of emigrant issues and politics, including the Council on American-Islamic Relations that works tirelessly in 19 states across the U.S. and has affiliates in Canada as well, advocating for the fair and equal treatment of the Muslim diaspora within North America.

Finally, the concept of decline allows for numerous options in Blumer's conception as adapted by Miller (1999), which are defined not by success or failure, but the disintegration of the social movement organization itself. Miller notes that there are four ways that social movements decline. Yet even the aforementioned options do not leave room for the festival-esque (Durkheim) feature of digital movements, without achieving their goals many of these movements are not co-opted or bureaucratized into a mainstream organization and are left to fester for months or years before reappearing on the scene (Hong Kong 2014 & 2015).

In considering the following chapters using Blumer's concepts, this chapter will update the stages of a social problem (movement) for digital era movements, as well as utilize Sökefeld's theory on diaspora movements to highlight the mobilization of marginalized communities. The first stage in contemporary social movement obviously follows Blumer in explaining the Emergence of the movement with an increased emphasis on the facilitation of information. It is arguable that emergence and awareness of the problem are separate stages in the digital age. Citizens are not waiting for a traditional, broadcast print model to coordinate information around. Information, gossip, dissent and ideology are circulating across the internet in real time, resulting in more quickly mobilized actions (see Rheingold 2003).

Contemporary sociopolitical movements bring public (local and global) awareness to injustices that are felt by the people in various types of regimes (democratic, semi-democratic, authoritarian). Protests can be distinguished from other categories of social movements those focused on regime change and sustained movements for change (or justice) by their emergence. Protests and riots are the least enduring of the social movement categories defined by this author but they are the most occurring (and spontaneous) movements globally, and can be the most effective in applying pressure for social change on governments. New social movement (NSM) theory are responses to massive social changes that were facilitated by globalization, tend to focus on matters of equality or quality of life issues, their organizational members tend to be composed of middle-income citizens as well as a strong infusion of the youth culture, and are fostered mainly via the internet and technology. This digital social mobilization provides for a nearly instantaneous reaction to breaking news, policy changes, or new circumstances – providing for spontaneity that traditional movements which did not have access to digital tools (such as Facebook and Twitter), lacked. Blumer concludes (1972, P. 68) that collective behavior in its elementary forms constitutes behavior that "arises spontaneously and is not due to pre-established understandings or traditions".

According to Snow and Moss (2014, P. 1128), spontaneity underlines many movements (predominately during the initial stages). They argue that this spontaneous nature of new movements is created by four specific conditions: "the absence of hierarchical organization; uncertain/ambiguous moments and events with a number of associated subconditions; behavioral/emotional priming and framing; and ecological/spatial contexts and constraints". The conditions for spontaneous collective action that Snow and Moss promulgate closely resemble those used to categorize new social movements in general, not simply one aspect of their development (see Gusfield, 1994). Protest movements in the digital era are occurring in a more spontaneous fashion due to organizational mobilization that is less dependent upon more formalized institutions or dissemination tactics that relied on a strong leader as well as communication tactics offered by the internet as a mobilization device.

Blumer argued that spontaneity is more likely to occur early in a movement's cycle (Emergence/Mobilization) than as it develops into a more organized entity (following his bureaucratization requirement). He noted, "It is at the outset that social movements bear their closest relationship to other forms of collective behavior. To the extent that social movements can ever be described as spontaneous or emergent, it is during this period" (Restated by Marx & McAdam, 1993, P. 73). However, again the nature of communicative mediums in the digital age allows for increased spontaneity for contemporary social (protest) movements lasting much longer than the *Emergence* period. A brief thought of the Arab Spring movement in Egypt offers renewed waves of spontaneity that changed the direction of the movement's goals from calls for increased transparency and reduced corruption among the military police to an outright call for the removal of Mubarak. The spontaneity there goes further with Muslims and Christians, men and women, business elites and the poor, coming together for a common political goal: regime change. As concluded by Snow and Moss (2014, P. 1138), "Spontaneous collective action can occur at various points in the career of protests and social movements, because the precipitating conditions with which spontaneity is most likely to be associated are not clustered at any single point in the career of these collective phenomena".

Snow and Moss (2014, P. 1123) are careful to note that spontaneous actions are not "random or unpredictable but rather that they are not premeditated or part of a formalized system of action". Yet unlike contagion theorists including Blumer and his mentor Mead, the impromptu action involved in new movements does not imply a lack of choice, cognition or rationality. Blumer (1939, P. 174) argued that social dissent was typically initiated by an event and spread through crowds, and from the crowds to the mass public, and led to "collective excitement" through observation of others to the stimuli. Actors are not participating in movements blindly, following the *hive mentality*. They are making decisions of risk and benefit in order to justify individual participation in a movement collective. Durkheim (1938) emphasized that the cognitive, emotional and moral experiences of the individual derive from social relations in groups.

Reeves and Bylund (1992, P. 115) note, "The co-participation of the performers of a ritual (collective action, movement) shapes the consciousness of each. The performers interact using symbolic representations and emotional displays to signify a common commitment to an idealized image of social structure". While the analysis of Durkheimian rituals is focused on religious festivals the concepts of collective action and behavior transcend just religious tradition into the sociopolitical realm and apply to the mobilization of movements. Durkheim typically characterizes the variations in solidarity associated with social movements as "intensifications of integrative bonds" (Trauggot, 1984, P. 325). In *Elementary Forms*, Durkheim argued that the increased levels of physical interaction combined with the increasing "ecological boundedness" of a protest group raise the intensity of collective emotions (Emirbayer, 2003, P. 14).

Collective or shared emotions generated in movements "crystallize into transpersonal patterns both of cultural or symbolic identification and of emotional commitment" (Emirbayer 2003, P. 14). In accordance with this statement as well as Durkheim's emphasis on the use of emblems or *sacred objects* of unity have become a renewed focal point for contemporary protest movements that adopt symbols, colors, or chants of social significance that provide a rallying point for protestors who are increasingly from different walks of life (umbrellas in Hong Kong; "We are Egypt" adopted from the Muslim Brotherhood slogan "We are Islam" during the Arab Spring movement). Blumer (1969, P. 11-12) also noted the importance of symbols or symbolic objects, noting "objects (in their sense of meaning) must be seen as social creations – as being formed in and arising out of the process of definition and interpretation as this process takes place in the interaction of people". Folk politics, or that which focuses on the local, direct actions that grassroots networks can take, rejects the concept of hegemony or (Srnicek & Williams, 2015), it embraces the festival over organization, and action over methodical coordination of goals and ideas. In effect, networked movements are at the Emergence stage characterized by their folk politics, or the realization that all politics is local and to spread awareness, thus mobilize, it must result from a genuine interest of citizens on the ground and spread organically upward from there.

Snow and Moss (2014, P. 1124) note spontaneous events "sometimes may be interconnected (individually and collectively), as when a spontaneous individual action stimulates a spontaneous collective action". Seemingly, and arguably, new social movements are able to spring up nearly out of the blue and sustain participation due to the lack of institutionalized ideologies as well as that these movements are not distinctly class or status-based. Thus, they are embracing more diverse populations who are equally affected by a social or political injustice or action by a regime that is widely perceived as illegitimate or non-representative. The dominating factor is the distribution of content (that will hopefully go viral), which leads to awareness and adherence to the movement, eventually developing into mobilization and actualization in the public sphere.

The second stage is Coalescence/Mobilization with a focus on the mobilization aspect because it is implied that the citizens have coalesced around an idea or movement if they have mobilized for it. Much like Blumer, this stage is defined by its reliance on communicative technologies (including SNS) to foster maximum participation from citizens. This stage is impacted by political opportunity theory, or the existence of an advantageous moment or event in a nation that makes mobilization of the masses more likely (Snow & Soule, 2010). As Snow and Soule explain, "whether individuals will act collectively to address their grievances depends in part on whether they have the political opportunity to do so" (2010, P. 66). Karatzogianni (2015, P. 98) argues that the most crucial impact of digital and communication technologies has been on political opportunity structures of social movements, allowing the swift emergence and mobilization of participants as well as the alignment and distribution of ideology, goals, and strategy. Mobilization techniques have been a strong focus of new social movement research because digital tools create questions surrounding effective mobilization and successful contemporary instances. This stage is concerned with increased awareness of the social problem and stimulation of the masses in order to effectively coordinate the third stage, transcendence or actualization of the movement.

The third stage proposed by this author replaces the requirement of Bureaucratization as suggested by Blumer. Piven and Cloward (1979) argue that as movement organizations bureaucratize, they reduce their effectiveness by turning from the political theatre of demonstration and protest that led to successful mobilization to more conventional actions through working within the system instead of outside. This point is particularly poignant in the age of digital protest. New social movements are no longer dependent on their incorporation into preexisting social movement and/or civil society organizations to succeed. According to Hohle (2010, P. 46), "All social movements occur within a territorial bounded system, and thus, have to negotiate with the constraints of normative civic codes located in the discourse of civil society", yet new social movements are eschewing traditional norms, codes, and organizations when fomenting dissent, which allows them to work beyond the civil society that may not always be willing to support protest.

Where the Bureaucratization stage is the critical stage for the progression of the social movement because it is the incorporation of elites, this is much more effectively observed in contemporary social movements in the second stage of coalescence. This puts an increased pressure on communicative mechanisms and citizen activists to use them to mobilize dissent quickly, which in occurring on various platforms that include the ability to stir emotionality with photos and videos as well as with basic text. This stimulation of the masses via the internet and social networking sites is characteristic of new social movements and the decentralized, bottom-up nature of the communicative technologies have an effect on the organization of the movement, making it less necessary for social movements to ordain leadership and further, to compromise their goals by bureaucratizing. The third stage as proposed by this author is known as Transcendence/Actualization and is characterized by the physical occupation of a square or space by the movement, transcending beyond the digital into the real. The concept of Transcendence/Actualization is also promulgated by Karatzogianni as she describes the "Revolutionary Virtual" or "the materialized mass of potentiality for change" (2015, P. 101).

Finally, the last stage is Decline which allows for movements that do not adhere to the four options proposed by Miller (1999) adapted from Blumer's work, such as festering and festival-like movements that have a resurgence of ideology and goals after the initial social movement. Theorists such as Macionis (2001) have suggested that there is an additional reason for the decline of social movements: establishment with the mainstream. The goals and/or ideologies of the social movement are adopted by the masses (arguably the reason Americans are still concerned with economic inequalities and the subsequent tension put on certain sectors of society long after the Occupy Wall Street movement faded into the background). Thus, there is no longer the need for the movement itself as it has been incorporated into popular dialogue. This is more likely the cause of decline in the #MeToo Movement, the greater pro-equal rights movement will likely be incorporated into the mainstream culture and the demonstrations as posited by Durkheim, exist in a state of arrested development (festival) until there is cause for mobilization. There is not bureaucratization of the movement by a larger entity or the government because it is the government the protestors are acting against. The institutionalization occurs among popular society instead of with a preexisting social movement organization – yet there are numerous cases in the digital age display that formalized bureaucratization or co-option are not always necessary in new social movements, when they are able to formalize and foment themselves across the mainstream populace using new technologies and communication platforms. This theme becomes evident in the #MeToo movement case study, which is undoubtedly a reawakening and rejuvenation of the waves of feminist movement of the 20th century in a new generation, who are fighting similar battles for equal rights in the 21st century.

For Sökefeld, the establishment of diaspora is an "issue of social mobilization" and borrowed from social movement theorists to explain the process by which diasporic movements are fomented. Sökefeld views social movements as "not completely institutionalized collectivities that lack formal representation, and that are engaged in contentious issues and interaction with opponents of various kinds", which is a simplified argument from Tilly and Tarrow (2007, etc.), but lends itself to the analysis of diaspora. Borrowing from prominent theories on social movements and mobilization, including political opportunity, framing/communicative theories, and resource mobilization, Sökefeld (2006, P. 270) characterizes the conditions that diasporic communities need to foment mobilization for sociopolitical change. He provides modes for mobilization of "transnationally dispersed people"; 1) opportunities in relation to the formation of diaspora (resources such as communication access, and protected freedoms such as speech and expression or the existence of a civil society that allows for dissent without reprisal); 2) providing for "mobilizing structures and practices" or forming a diasporic community network to disseminate ideology and movement goals. Sökefeld notes that these networks may exist at the local level (personal interactions, face-to-face mobilization) or because of the transnational nature of diasporic communities, at an international level via "kinship ties"; 3) framing the community identity, which includes "all the ideas from which an imagination of community is composed, the ideas that define migrants as members of a transnational community or relationships of belonging", which brings the concept of collective identity back into focus. Belonging denotes how membership in a group (diaspora or social movement network) demands participation in various political performances (displays of dissent) (Bell, 1999). These en masse performances are crucial to establishing the necessary connections between individuals, collective identities, locations, and remembering (shared memories, heritage, norms).

Sökefeld views diaspora as a social form (in the Vertovec definition) and details how an imagined community of displaced peoples are able to provide for a collective identity and the structures that are necessary for mobilization in the broader society. Highlighting his own work on the Alevi Movement in Germany, Sökefeld notes the formation of an imagined transnational community (diaspora) based around the Alevi (religious/ethnic minority group), and arguably other diasporic populations (e.g., the Kurds) is not just a result of migration but also occurs in "response to specific issues in both the country of residence and the country of origin that bore no relation to the original movement of migration" (2006, P. 274). The politics of acknowledgement or recognition can play a major role in coalescing a diasporic collective identity and mobilizing that collective identity for greater rights within the host country (and often, its political system). Sökefeld (2006, P. 275) notes, "the opportunity for deferred emergence of diaspora is a consequence of technological innovation...because of the emergence of a transnational imagination community as a result of critical events requires that such events are globally communicated". The digital age and its technologies (including the internet infrastructure) have increased the opportunities for diasporic populations to reach beyond their local community and create a transnational network to discuss issues of political, religious, cultural, and economic importance as well as share experiences from the host country and country of origin.

From a framing theory perspective, Sökefeld and Schwalgin (2000) argue that in order for a transnational collective identity to form the imagined community must become a reality, in terms of organizing associations, groups, and foster networks in which to share the diasporic community's ideology and goals for mobilization. Framing theory argues that social movements put their ideology into strategic frames, which make the message and goals more digestible (and easier to commit to) for potential participants in the movement (Snow et al., 1986; McAdam et al., 1996; McCammon et al., 2007). It is through the personal interactions that an individual has within the collective diasporic (or social movement) identity that mobilization foments and through proper framing provides for sustainability of the dissent and diasporic identity. Davies (2000) pointedly notes, "The experience of being a person is captured through the notion of subjectivity as constituted through discourses. Integral to these discourses are desires, specific histories, fragmentation, contradiction, discontinuities and embodied ways of knowing, that importantly the individual is constituted through the discourses of a number of collectives as the collective itself" (P. 57). However, Sökefeld is careful to warn that once diasporic communities are established does not mean that community is going to exist in perpetuity in the same form, but "have to be reproduced time and again in order to continue" to be "politically and socially effective" (2006, P. 276).

Blumer and Sökefeld intertwine on the concept of mobilization (or coalescence of a movement) both noting the importance of awareness of the social problem/issue (framing) and the participation of a broad swathe of the community, this is also important during the decline of a movement in terms of how the movement's goals and ideology are incorporated into the mainstream population. Again this author will diverge from both authors on the concept of institutionalization or bureaucratization as being a necessity for contemporary social (diaspora) movements to mobilize and sustain protest. The emergence and coalescence of social movements in the digital age presupposes an individual who is exposed to the ideology for and against the movement to have co-signed or agreed (or not) to participate in the collective action, as opposed to needing two separate steps for emergence and coalescence, this author argues that once a networked individual becomes aware of a social issue they decide almost immediately whether or not they believe in the change being advocated, etc. (as explained previously).

Sökefeld concludes, "Mobilization for diaspora need not be a straightforward process but can be intersected by other social and political processes that may be related to competing identifications. The process of diasporic mobilization is frequently disturbed and impeded by intervening action, crosscutting identifications and conflicting interests" (2006, P. 279). The diasporic community tends to be more susceptible to contradicting (or too varied) agendas, but through the establishment of a diasporic identity/consciousness is better suited than a lot of social movement organizations at providing a foundation of ideology to foment dissent. Sökefeld emphasizes, "The assumption of a shared identity that unites people living dispersed in transnational space thereby becomes the central defining feature of diasporas" (2006, P. 280), and is an important factor to the mobilization of a diaspora. This sentiment is reiterated by Abramson (2017) in the argument regarding "diasporization", or the "strategic attempt to construct a diasporic identity" in order to cultivate a shared identity that transcends borders (P. 15). Abramson develops the diasporization theory by accepting a central tenant of diasporic identity construction, which is that it is based on a history of displacement from a homeland and the maintenance of a narrative of attachment to that homeland. Thus, "diasporization refers to the process, through which scattered individuals become part of an imagined collectivity oriented towards a real or imagined homeland" (Abramson, 2017, P. 15).

## NEW SOCIAL MOVEMENT LITERATURE: A BRIEF SUMMARY

As noted with Blumer and Sökefeld, for social movements to foster the presence of a there needs to be an opportunity for dissent to foment, which entails both factors of the civil society (most importantly, the ability for citizens to engage in dialogue and assembly without interference from the regime) and psychological factors (often a shared sense of oppression or a mutual goal). Theorists tend to focus on the psychological aspects to fomenting mobilization and the 'rational choice' to participate, yet this text seeks to unravel more engrained psychological factors to diaspora social movement participation. Rogers, Goldstein, and Fox (2018) argue that "self-sacrifice" is inherent to collective action, to the contrary of Olson's theory of rational choice, the authors note that one should expect for sociopolitical mobilization to cost a participant something (time, resources, etc.). Yet the authors go onto explain that this sacrifice is for the greater good. Contemporary sociopolitical mobilization is quite often associated with egalitarian and lofty goals, which require participants to work on behalf of others or the Other in society. The new age has also seen a revitalization of old-school tactics, such as the boycott or sit-in that have been digitized as well as conducted in the public sphere. These tactics necessitate the participation of more than a single individual – as they become more effective the greater the number of participants boycotting a store/company, or in the case of a digital sit-in it requires as many people as possible accessing a website simultaneously causing a distributed denial of service (DDoS) attack rendering the website ineffective and unresponsive.

The psychological aspects of collective action are often highlighted by speaking about emotion or the affective nature of mobilization, not just motivation, (often anger at a policy action or inaction or perceived injustice) but self-gratification that comes from advocating on behalf of something one believes. This may be best highlighted by the tribalism in American politics today via social media platforms, it takes one glance at a trending topic (or hashtag) regarding Donald Trump to see extreme polarization coupled with intense emotion for and against the man and the administration's policies.

Klandermans and de Weerd (2000, P. 76) note that "collective action participation presupposes the existence of grievances, of feelings of injustice..." In a similar manner, Montada and Schneider (1989) argue that emotions (such as rage or guilt) may contribute to an individual's willingness to participate in social mobilization, while Jasper (1998) and Eyerman (2006) assert that emotions often encourage membership/participation in a social movement, solidify bonds among members, and assist in framing the message for the mainstream audience.

This could account for the large number of male participants in the Women's Marches or speaking out on social media using hashtags such as #AllMenCan (White, 2014) and #MeToo to discuss their relationships with women in attempt to absolve themselves of affiliation with the bad actors, most often citing their daughters. The interactions involved in contemporary social mobilization are more personal (in terms of intimacy of the political/social issue being advocated) and transcendent (in terms of reach of ideology and mobilization tactics), making them arguably more effective than traditional mobilization that stayed localized. While there are arguments that digital communication platforms such as Facebook and Twitter make social mobilization less personal, these tools enable emotive content to produce affective response from populations both home and abroad.

Rogers, Goldstein, and Fox (2018, P. 360) outline a behavioral code regarding collective action, they dub the code PANIC, and argue "social mobilization efforts tend to be more effective when they are" 1) *Personal* (or involve personal interaction with like-minded people; 2) *Accountable* (or making people's behavior public in order for them to feel that their action or inaction could have consequences for them personally); 3) *Normative* (conveying what people of influence should do); 4) *Identity relevant* (aligning behaviors with the way people actually perceive themselves or would like to see themselves); and 5) *Connected* (which involves leveraging the structure of people's networks and the platforms that maintain those networks). The authors focus wholly on the affective response elicited from participants via collective action at a personal level (face-to-face) rather than focusing on the networked interactions that have increasingly become an important factor to contemporary mobilization. New social movement theories note that movement collective identity is "expressed in everyday activities of movement members and that relationships to networks external to movements reinforce network commitments and ideology", which means that protest activities are increasingly more incorporated into our daily lives, such as boycotting a certain store or brand (Stryker, 2000, P. 29). Contemporary activists on the whole remain committed to the social/political change that they are advocating for by joining social movements, which has impacts on their personal lives and interactions beyond the social movement network (Andrews, 1991; McAdam, 1988). Personal interactions color the protest community with demonstrations, rallies, and marches in the streets, and foster "perceived similarit[ies] among those participating in such events – such as similarity in perceived identity (e.g., women) or even clothing (e.g., wearing a knitted pink hat) – can foster social bonds among them (Rogers, Goldstein, & Fox, 2018, P. 364).

People are more likely to conform to sociopolitical action/policy if they share a social identity reference point that is associated with that norm, this is evident in the #MeToo movement as more high profile women come forward to express their personal experiences of sexual assault and harassment, women at all socioeconomic levels are becoming more comfortable about confronting the subjugator in their lives. This also relates to the principle of identity relevant in social mobilization where people are more likely to participate in dissent with people they share similarities. Snow and McAdams (2000) assert that the coalescence of a movement and participation of those who already identify with it is *identity convergence.* The authors argue,

*personal identities are isomorphic or congruent with the collective identity of a movement, such that the existence of a movement provides an avenue for the individual to act in accordance with his or her personal identity...the problem is one of connection and thus the specification of the mechanisms that facilitate the convergence of parallel individual identities with a movement and its collective identity. (Snow & McAdams, P. 47)*

Rogers, Goldstein, and Fox promulgate the existence of two identity types, social and self. Social identities "encompass people's perceptions and beliefs about social groups with which they have an emotional identification...the influence of social group identification on behavior depends on both the strength of a person's identification with the social group and on the social identity's salience at the moment of behavior is to be performed" (2018, P. 370). Social identity theory was most notably promulgated by Tajfel (1981) who defines social identity as "that part of the individual's self-concept which derives from his knowledge of his membership in a social group(s) together with the value and emotional significance attached to that membership" (P. 225). Social mobilization is more effective at fomenting dissent and participation when the movement emphasizes a threat to a social identity. Self-identities encompass how people perceive themselves, and typically collective action that is based on self-identity are able to use people's natural motivation to see themselves positively (Leary, 2007). Self-categorization or identity theory developed from Turner et al. (1987), and is characterized by reasoned groupings of oneself. Collective action, as promulgated by this author, necessitates both the social and self-identity or the concept of the networked collective, where participants in digital social movements are able to maintain their individuality and personal ideologies while advocating for the greater good.

New social movement theory emphasizes the importance of identity and the shared beliefs that make collective action foment (Melucci, 1985). According to Johnston, Larana, and Gusfield (1994, P. 15), "The concept of collective identity refers to the (often implicitly) agreed upon definition of membership, boundaries, and activities for the group." Thus collective identity is developed and sustained through the interactions and networks within the social movement as well as diasporic communities and organizations. Collective identity remains critical for social movement mobilization and the movement's ability to achieve its stated goal based on the collective amassed for protest. Rogers, Goldstein, and Fox note the "ultimate goal" of social mobilization is "often to motivate citizens to engage in relatively difficult, time-consuming, or costly actions, where the psychological barrier to initial participation is fairly high" (2018, P. 372).

Thus, framing the issue becomes important if mobilization is dependent upon an affective or psychological stimulant. Arguably social movement organizations (or influencers, if organization is lacking) are key to providing motivation to join the protest and coalescing a movement around an established, or stated goal. Social connection, both on-and-offline is also a crucial factor to mobilization. As previously stated, digital tools empower citizens to engage in sociopolitical dissent and are a vital incubator of said dissent, particularly social media platforms. As Rogers, Goldstein, and Fox assert, "How personally connected two individuals feel affects the influence they exert on each other", which invokes Granovetter's (1973) seminal thesis on the strength of one's network ties. As Koinova (2016, P. 502) notes, "Core mobilization efforts take place through mobilizing structures of tight identity-based networks rooted in family, neighborhood, and private ties...This definition emphasizes diaspora engagement with the homeland-oriented dimension."

Yet Granovetter's theory needs updating for the age of social media, yet it remains salient, stating that individuals who share a close connection, or strong tie (family, close friends) are more influenced by those strong ties than weak ones (colleagues, coworkers). Yet in the social media age, researchers must account for influencers or those who have an established name (sometimes for nothing, e.g., Logan Paul) and a dedicated following of what Granovetter would consider weak ties, as they are not often actors who are personally known by the influencer. While these influencers may not have as much power over individuals as people within their immediate circle, on social or political issues, influencers can be critical catalysts for many to participate in a movement (Rose McGowan and #MeToo; Joshua Wong and the Umbrella Movement, Hong Kong 2014; etc.). Yet it is still important for the development and sustainability of a social movement to not just target influencers and their networks but also populations on the fringe of the network (including diasporic populations). To conclude this author turns to Ragazzi (2012, P. 109), who summarizes, "Whether diaspora is understood as a social movement, a signifier, or a political discourse, a processual approach to diaspora takes a different starting point, considering diaspora to be not only the end result but also the process through which a particular social and political reality is produced." Theorists analyzing diaspora politics and mobilization in the digital age will need to take on an increasingly comparative, process-driven method to flesh out the unique characteristic of individual diasporic communities, the creation of a collective identity, maintenance of transnational diasporic networks, and fomenting of diasporic mobilization.

The following chapter provides a background into the selected cases of collective action, detailing the political, social, and media environment leading to the instance of protest or revolution. Following the tradition of historical institutionalism, it is essential in developing or contributing to the overall theory of new social movements (or any topic) to understand the context and history in which these movements coalesced. The case studies will also be detailed and the author will provide justification for choosing the thematic approach to dissecting contemporary diaspora politics in terms of politically (territorial) versus psychologically (affect/sentiment).

## REFERENCES

Abramson, Y. (2017). Making a homeland, constructing a diaspora: The case of Taglit-Birthright Israel. *Political Geography, 58*, 14–23. doi:10.1016/j.polgeo.2017.01.002

Batliwala, S., & Brown, L. (2006). *Transnational Civil Society: An Introduction*. University of Michigan: Kumarian Press.

Blumer, H. (1939). Collective Behavior. In R. E. Park (Ed.), *An Outline of the Principles of Sociology* (pp. 219–280). New York: Barnes & Noble.

Blumer, H. (1955). Reflections on Theory of Race Relations. In A. W. Lind (Ed.), *Race Relations in World Perspective* (pp. 3–21). Honolulu, HI: University of Hawaii Press.

Blumer, H. (1969). *Symbolic Interactionism: Perspective and Method.* Englewood Cliffs, NJ: Prentice-Hall.

Blumer, H. (1971). Social Problems as Collective Behavior. *Social Problems, 18*(Winter), 298–306. doi:10.2307/799797

Davies, B. (2000). *A Body of Writing*. Walnut Creek, CA: AltaMira Press.

Della Porta, D., & Diani, M. (2006). *Social Movements: An Introduction* (2nd ed.). Oxford, UK: Blackwell Publishing.

Emirbayer, M. (Ed.). (2003). *Emile Durkheim: Sociologist of Modernity.* Oxford, UK: Blackwell Publishing.

Granovetter, M. (1973). The Strength of Weak Ties. *American Journal of Sociology, 78*(6), 1360–1380. doi:10.1086/225469

Gusfield, J. (1994). The Reflexivity of Social Movements: Collective Behavior and Mass Society Theory Revised. In E. Larana, H. Johnston, & J. Gusfield (Eds.), *New Social Movements: From Ideology to Identity* (pp. 58–79). Philadelphia: Temple University Press.

Hohle, R. (2010). Politics, Social Movements, and the Body. *Sociology Compass, 4*(1), 38–51. doi:10.1111/j.1751-9020.2009.00260.x

Karatzogianni, A. (2015). *Firebrand Waves of Digital Activism 1994-2014: The Rise and Spread of Hacktivism and Cyberconflict*. Palgrave MacMillan. doi:10.1057/9781137317933

Klandermans, B., & de Weerd, M. (2000). Group identification and political protest. In S. Stryker, T. J. Owens, & R. W. White (Eds.), Social movements, protest, and contention; v. 13. Self, identity, and social movements (pp. 68-90). Minneapolis, MN: University of Minnesota Press.

Koinova, M. (2016). Sustained vs episodic mobilization among conflict-generated diasporas. *International Political Science Review*, *37*(4), 500–516. doi:10.1177/0192512115591641

Leary, M. (2007). Motivational and Emotional Aspects of the Self. *Annual Review of Psychology*, *58*(1), 317–344. doi:10.1146/annurev.psych.58.110405.085658 PMID:16953794

Macionis, J. J. (2001). *Sociology* (8th ed.). Prentice Hall.

Marx, G., & McAdams, D. (1993). *Collective Behavior and Social Movements: Process and Structure*. London: Pearson PLC.

Melucci, A. (1985). The symbolic challenge of contemporary movements. *Social Research*, *52*, 789–816.

Miller, F. D. (1999). The end of SDS and the emergence of weatherman: Demise through success. In J. Freeman & V. Johnson (Eds.), *Waves of protest: Social movements since the Sixties* (pp. 303–324). Rowman & Littlefield Publishers.

Montada, L., & Schneider, A. (1989). Justice and Emotional Reactions to the Disadvantaged. *Social Justice Research*, *3*(4), 313–344. doi:10.1007/BF01048081

Piven, F., & Cloward, R. (1979). *Poor People's Movements: Why They Succeed, How They Fail*. New York: Vintage Books.

Ragazzi, F. (2012). Diaspora: The Politics of Its Meanings. *International Political Sociology*, *6*(1), 107–111. doi:10.1111/j.1749-5687.2011.00152_5.x

Reeves, E., & Bylund, R. (1992). Anonymity and the Rise of Universal Occasions for Religious Ritual: An Extension of the Durkheimian Theory. *Journal for the Scientific Study of Religion*, *31*(2), 113. doi:10.2307/1387003

Rheingold, H. (2003). *Smart mobs: The next social revolution*. Cambridge, MA: Basic Books.

Rogers, T., Goldstein, N., & Fox, C. (2018). Social Mobilization. *Annual Review of Psychology*, *69*(1), 357–381. doi:10.1146/annurev-psych-122414-033718 PMID:28945979

Snow, D., & McAdam, D. (2000). Identity Work Processes in the Context of Social Movements: Clarifying the Identity/Movement Nexus. In S. Stryker, T. J. Owens, & R. W. White (Eds.), *Self, identity, and social movements* (pp. 41–68). Minneapolis, MN: University of Minnesota Press.

Snow, D., & Moss, D. (2014). Protest on the Fly: Toward a Theory of Spontaneity in the Dynamics of Protest and Social Movements. *American Sociological Review*, *79*(6), 1122–1143. doi:10.1177/0003122414554081

Snow, D., & Soule, S. (2010). *A Primer on Social Movements*. New York: W.W. Norton.

Sökefeld, M. (2006). Mobilizing in transnational space: A social movement approach to the formation of diaspora. *Global Networks*, *6*(3), 265–284. doi:10.1111/j.1471-0374.2006.00144.x

Sökefeld, M., & Schwalgin, S. (2000). *Institutions and their Agents in Diaspora: A Comparison of Armenians in Athens and Alevis in Germany*. Presented at the 6th European Association of Social Anthropologists Conference, Krakau. Accessed from: http://www.transcomm.ox.ac.uk/working%20papers/schwal.pdf

Srnicek, N., & Williams, A. (2015). *Inventing the Future: Postcapitalism and a World Without Work*. London: Verso Books.

Stryker, S. (2000). Identity Competition: Key to Differential Social Movement Participation? In S. Stryker, T. J. Owens, & R. W. White (Eds.), *Self, identity, and social movements* (pp. 21–41). Minneapolis, MN: University of Minnesota Press.

Tajfel, H. (1981). *Human Groups and Social Categories: Studies in Social Psychology*. Cambridge, UK: Cambridge University Press.

Tilly, C., & Tarrow, S. (2007). *Contentious politics*. Boulder, CO: Paradigm Publishers.

Traugott, M. (1984). Durkheim and Social Movements. *Archives Européennes de Sociologie*, *25*(02), 319–326. doi:10.1017/S000397560000429X

Turner, J. C. (1987). The Analysis of Social Influence. In J. C. Turner, M. A. Hogg, P. J. Oakes, S. D. Riecher, & M. S. Wetherell (Eds.), *Rediscovering the Social Group: A Self- Categorization Theory* (pp. 68–88). Oxford, UK: Blackwell.

Weber, M. (1978). *Economy and Society: An Outline of Interpretive Sociology*. Berkley, CA: University of California Press.

# Chapter 3
# Methodological Considerations and Explanation of Case Studies


## ABSTRACT

*This chapter examines various definitions of diaspora and how the characterization of diaspora has evolved over time and through adoption in fields beyond international relations. The chapter provides an explanation on historical institutionalism, which is adopted by the author to explain the selected case studies as well as provides greater insight into the social movement and symbolic interactionism theories of Herbert Blumer, which are used widely in diaspora studies and sociological theories on identity construction. The chapter provides justification for the author's use of qualitative analysis and methods of researching diaspora.*


## INTRODUCTION

Scholarship on diaspora has changed dramatically since the time when the concept was primarily applied to historical diasporas, such as the Jews, the Greeks, or the Armenians. Additionally, while the study of diasporas was traditionally more popular among scholars of history and anthropology, in the past two decades it has received increasingly more attention by economists and political scientists, seeking to challenge traditional conceptions of dispersed groups and their perceived (often negative) impact on a host country. Diaspora

DOI: 10.4018/978-1-5225-7757-7.ch003

Copyright © 2019, IGI Global. Copying or distributing in print or electronic forms without written permission of IGI Global is prohibited.

research has evolved into transnational considerations of cultural identity and seeks to explain more than simply an attachment to a homeland (real or perceived). The concepts of *old* and *new* diaspora are detailed in Chapter Six, yet it is worth noting that contemporary (new) diaspora are better equipped than classical (old) diaspora to facilitate communities and discourse among scattered populations. New diaspora are situated within the digital age, which is characterized by its transnational nature, leaving theorists of contemporary diaspora with a responsibility to both explain the shifting role of the nation-state while making certain not to completely neglect its importance in fostering a collective diasporic identity. Delano and Gamlen (2014, P. 45) note, "State-diaspora relations are a clear example of transnationalism: they involve states spilling across their borders in search of their own people. While some commentators look dimly upon this as a form of long distance ethnic nationalism, others herald it as part of the emergence of emancipatory post-national, supranational and transnational forms of citizenship."

Brubaker (2005) argues that the old (classical) characterization of diaspora was "immigrationist, assimilationist, (methodologically) nationalist, teleological...The new perspective does not make these assumptions. It is said to 'transcend' the old assimilationist, immigrationist paradigm" (P. 8). In analyzing the transnational and digital nature of contemporary diaspora and the accompanying politics, diasporic community influencers have co-opted the concept of diaspora and changed it from "descriptive to prescriptive", it [diaspora] has been used by influencers to mobilize dispersed populations in order to foster diasporic network connections, build and sustain diasporic community organizations, and mobilize political action, which is now taking place at a local, national, and transnational level. The digital facilitation of discourse and sharing of information (heritage, ideology, etc.) among the diasporic community and beyond allows "dispersed Diasporas [to] gain political and community visibility" (Georgiou, 2002, P. 2). It is the digital public sphere that keeps issues in the mainstream public's awareness as well as diasporic community members across the world.

In relation to contemporary methods of analyzing diaspora, Kissau and Hunger argue that digital methods such as content or network analysis would be helpful in deciphering the sustainability of diasporic networks online. The authors note,

*By evaluating ongoing changes in the communication practices and characteristics of internet sites, however, the fluidity and malleability of transnational structures and relations can be taken into account. For example, using network analysis of linkage structures of different communities within the internet, the contact to other actors can be traced and shifts in activism and orientation can be monitored. (2008, P. 14)*

The research, and more specifically, the case studies presented in this work have been examined through a comparative qualitative scope. The work uses historical institutionalism as a method of dissecting the foundation of the selected movements as well as ethnography in the form of primary interviews with members of a diasporic community in the United States to better highlight unique stories of gender and belonging. The choice to employ historical institutionalism to cases of new social movements is an important feature of this work, it is crucial to provide thorough explanations as to the historical, economic, political, social, and cultural underpinnings of each new movement or instance of collective action. This is the best way to not only explain the differences and similarities in networked movements, but also to contribute to an overarching theory of how these movements coalesce, sustain, and decline.

The use of qualitative methods over quantitative is one that this author believes helps to better inform the work as well as the reader regarding new social movements that are using digital technologies to mobilize. Quantitative methods such as content analysis or the use of metadata from social media sites to construct a timeline of posts to better highlight the emergence and mobilization phases of movements would enrich case studies, particularly those that examine affective response. Yet the research questions addressed in this work pertain to the use of digital tools and the internet to both mobilize social movements, but also how those tools are making the necessity of a more formalized organization questionable, as these networked movements are more effective at self-bureaucratizing. Thus it is crucial to this work to not construct maps and charts that explain nodes of communication and influencers in the selected instances of collective action, but to provide a deep understanding of how these movements began and the politics and society preceding, during, and after the action.

## QUALITATIVE METHODS AND COMPARATIVE POLITICS

The use of qualitative methods, according to Mahoney (2007, P. 125), is two-fold: in some cases, analysts will use qualitative methodology to explain cases that deviate from the norm or accepted theories; in other cases (such as this thesis), qualitative methods are used comparatively to "formulate new hypotheses" (Mahoney 2007, P. 125). Theorists dating back to the mid-1970s have used multiple case studies to juxtapose, finding commonalities and differences on varied topics in political science, such as democratization (i.e.: Collier, 1999; Huntington, 1991), electoral politics (Collier & Collier, 1991), and of course, social movements (Goodwin, 2001; McAdam, Tarrow, & Tilly, 2001). An important distinction between quantitative and qualitative methods is that the latter can be used to uncover intricacies, such as feelings, thought processes, and mobilization stimuli that are extremely difficult to extrapolate using statistics and numbers (Strauss & Corbin, 1998).

Mahoney and Goertz (2006, P. 230) note that qualitative theorists begin with cases and their outcomes (or mechanisms/processes that contribute to the outcome), and construct explanations of the causes moving backward, adopting a "causes-of-effects" approach. This argument is consistent with this author's line of thinking methodologically and is evident in the case studies analyzed in this work. Again, qualitative comparative analysis of selected instances of collective action through the lens of historical institutionalism (which will be explained in the next section), provides for a more thorough understanding of the foundation of these movements, protests, or revolutions, as well as the political and media environment in which they take place. Blumler et al. note,

*At the level of observation, comparative inquiry cosmopolitanizes, opening our eyes to communication patterns and problems unnoticeable in our spatial and temporal milieu. It helps us to see our communication arrangements in a fresh light, enriches the raw material sources of communication theory building, and deepens appreciation of communication policy issues, learning how they have arisen and been dealt with in other places and periods. (1992, P. 30)*

As diaspora studies and research on diasporic communities continues into the digital age, it becomes increasingly important that theorists are analyzing these communities not as singular entities of displacement and dissent, but from an individual community level in order to better understand the similarities and difference among and between diasporic populations. According to Mahoney and Goertz, "From the qualitative perspective, the assessment of necessary and/or sufficient causation seems quite natural and fully consistent with logic and good science" (2006, P. 232). This is the perspective from which this thesis is informed and attempts to provide answers as to the fomenting of dissent within networked diasporic movements that result in collective action.

There are various paradigms in qualitative research that can be applied to examine a multitude of inquiries in political science, including social movements and collective action, which are explored in this thesis. According to the paradigm positions presented by Guba and Lincoln (1994), the cases in this work are presented using critical theory (including historical institutionalism, new social movement theory, and ethnography) through the voice of a "transformative intellectual as advocate and activist" using "structural/historical insights" via case study analysis (P. 112). The authors note that the "aim of inquiry [in critical theory] is the critique and transformation of the social, political, cultural, economic, ethnic and gender structures that constrain and exploit humankind, by engagement in confrontation, even conflict... Advocacy and activism are key concepts" (Guba & Lincoln, 1994, P. 113).

To reiterate, there was a conscious decision by the author to focus on qualitative rather than quantitative methods in highlighting the selected cases, which were chosen to highlight differences and similarities among instances of networked collective action. While there are methods that would combine methods such as content analysis, the intention of this work is to construct an updated framework of thinking regarding diaspora and social movements in the digital age, which requires a deeper understanding of the individual cases that qualitative methods are best suited to provide. Numbers or quantifying communications do not explain the underlying problems within a nation or society that lead to collective action, nor are they able on their own to construct a complete picture of mood, symbolism, stakes, or goals of a movement. Numbers are also not able to convey what it feels like to not belong in one's society due to diaspora politics and the Othering within host societies, which is why this author chose to take an ethnographic approach to Chapter Four by conducting interviews with female members of the Muslim diasporic community in the U.S. to provide a greater awareness of not just the surface level politics, but the emotion that is involved in migration and resettling.

In using qualitative methods, it is common to narrowly focus on theories and make inferences that are generalizable in limited cases. Qualitative methods tend to start with selecting cases where outcomes of interest have occurred, and work to explain the circumstances, stimuli, and action that led to said outcome through techniques such as personal interviews, vigorous use of secondary sources, and crafting case studies. Qualitative Comparative Analysis (QCA) is used as a research approach in this thesis and "refers to the iterative process of data collection, model specification, case selection and re-conceptualization of the conditions and the outcome which are of central importance for any QCA-based research design" (Wagemann & Scheider, 2010, P. 2). Using qualitative techniques allows for a more informed consciousness and the ability to decipher how situations (political, economic, cultural, etc.) may be changed, as Giroux (1988, P. 213) notes, "To uncover and excavate those forms of historical and subjugated knowledges that point to experiences of suffering, conflict, and collective struggle…to link the notion of historical understanding to elements to critique and hope."

## HISTORICAL INSTITUTIONALISM AND NEW SOCIAL MOVEMENTS

Historical institutionalism is a relatively new method in social science (notably, sociology and political science) that focuses on institutions to find patterns in social and political change over time. Pierson and Skocpol (2002, P. 1) state, "Historical institutionalists analyze organizational configurations where others look at particular settings in isolation; and they pay attention to critical junctures and long-term processes where others look only at slices of time or short-term maneuvers". The cases selected in this work are examined using historical institutionalism, with a focus on the media, political, and social environment long before the collective action moment of interest. There is a close examination on institutional organizations within the social movements as well as a focus on whether the movement necessitated more formal ties with pre-established institutions (government or civil society).

Historical institutionalism as a method seeks to uncover and understand the "overarching contexts and interacting processes that shape and reshape states, politics, and public policymaking" (Pierson & Skocpol, 2007, P. 1), using a multitude of approaches, some institutionalists will use primary sources, while others analyze findings from secondary sources (as is the approach in this work). Pierson and Skocpol (2007, P. 3) address three features that characterize historical institutionalism research in political science:

1. Historical institutionalists address "big, substantive questions that are inherently of interest to broad publics as well as to fellow scholars";
2. Historical institutionalists "take time seriously" and seek to trace the roots of a political change, the events leading to the change, and do account for temporality quite intently;
3. Historical institutionalists "analyze macro contexts and hypothesize about the combined effects of institutions and processes rather than examining just one institution or process at a time".

The focus in using historical institutionalism as a method is on "explaining variations in important or surprising patterns, events, or arrangements – rather than on accounting for human behavior without regard to context or modeling very general processes presumed to apply at all times and places" (Pierson & Skocpol, 2007, P. 4). The emphasis is on building context and awareness of a state, a body politic, and/or sociopolitical tensions before, during, and after the analyzed event (an election, revolution, protest, etc.). The case studies of interest in this work have been dissected using historical institutionalism to underline the national, political, and social context in each *phase* of movement. Each case study is presented using qualitative comparative analysis as well as historical institutionalism to provide a rich background of social movement organization and the diasporic communities involved. As Pierson and Skocpol note, "Efforts to systematically trace social processes can make an essential contribution to supporting or challenging claims about social causation" (2007, P. 6). Thus adding to the volumes on social movement theory, and more recently networked movements using available technologies to organize protest.

Theorists such as Skocpol (1979) and Goodwin (2001) have taken advantage of historical institutionalism in developing literature on revolutions, first by analyzing success and failure in revolutions occurring within Central America and East Asia, and then emphasizing the varied conditions and actors that aided in mobilization in each region. Pierson and Skocpol (2007, P. 18) succinctly argue that a "scholar who wants to understand revolutions is unlikely to be willing to start with a purely random set of times and places; she will want to make sure that clear-cut revolutions are included in her research…It has long been standard to test hypotheses with comparisons between "positive cases" where phenomena of interest occur and closely matched "negative cases" where phenomena do not occur". Following this characterization, the cases selected for this research consider how diasporic communities are formed and around what (psychological/affective lines or territorial/homeland ties). The cases were chosen to highlight two stratified ways of defining diaspora, politically (or territorially) and psychologically, as well as geographic differences, and populations with varied identities.

## SYMBOLIC INTERACTIONISM AND SOCIAL MOVEMENT MOBILIZATION

Herbert Blumer (1900-1987) is a sociologist by practice but is most commonly associated with his work on *symbolic interactionism*, a theory that combined elements of philosophy, psychology, and sociology. Though George Herbert Mead (one of Blumer's mentors and advisors) created the approach in his theories of social behaviorism, it was Blumer who coined the term symbolic interactionism in 1937 (Hallet et al., 2009). Interactionists have a focus on internal processes of organizations, yet their main concerns are "the relationships among individuals and how people create meanings and social relations" (Hallet et al., 2009, P. 3). While symbolic interactionism was not widely recognized until the 1960s culminating in a collection of Blumer's writings being published in 1969, Blumer developed himself as a collective behavior scholar at the University of Chicago Department of Sociology (Hallet et al., 2009; Weber & King, 2014). Blumer was particularly interested in the affective and social processes that lead to collective or shared awareness and the facilitation of mobilization.

Blumer noted in 1947 that organizational sociology does not consider human actors as useful or necessary, noting:

*It must visualize human beings as acting, striving, calculating, sentimental and experiencing persons and not as the automatons and neutral agents implied by the more dominant of our current scientific ideologies and methodologies... It must embrace the complicated behavior of these collectivities, particularly as they act and prepare to act toward one another. (1947, P. 277)*

Hallet et al. (2009) argue that the interactionism espoused by Mead and Blumer as well as the Second Chicago School, including writings by Erving Goffman and Howard Becker allowed researchers to bring the people back into focus as a functional piece of social change. Blumer's principles of symbolic interactionism were disseminated and promulgated by students who took his classes at the University of Chicago, at which he became faculty in 1931, and influenced sociologist such as Gusfield. Blumer argued that much of human activity takes the form of symbolic interaction, meaning that the event or "interaction in which we interpret the acts of others and the meanings of objects, and then respond on the basis of those interpretations and meanings" (1936, P. 518; 1969, P. 537). Blumer stated:

*The symbolic interactionists view social interaction as primarily a communicative process in which...a person responds not to what another individual says or does, but to the meaning of what he says or does. Their view, consequently, might be regarded as inserting a middle term of interpretation into the stimulus-response couplet so that it becomes stimulus-interpretation-response. (Blumer 1937, P. 171)*

In his work Blumer also consider non-symbolic interaction, which is characterized by the "unconscious responses that one makes to the gestures of others" (1936, P. 519), this argument lead to theories of crowd mentality or group think where actions are spontaneous yet direct. For Blumer (1969), it is the role of the theorist to explain how structures (including organizations and social processes) impact the process of symbolic interaction (or how they are interpreted for an individual, group, or society). Blumer rejected both idealism and realism as leading to unacceptable theories – leaning toward the fantastical on one end, and viewing the world and its structures as fixed on the other. This rejection further informs his position as a symbolic interactionist, for Blumer, "action and the creation of meaning are in an ever-emergent situated present that is cognitively, behaviorally, and intersubjectively inseparable from the past and the future" (Morroine, 2004, P. xii).

Stets and Burke (2003, P. 4) take a symbolic interactionism approach to their analysis of construction of self-identity, noting,

*When one's self is encapsulated as a set of symbols to which one may respond to itself as an object, as it responds to any other symbol, the self has emerged. The hallmark of this process – of selfhood – is reflexivity. Humans have the ability to reflect back upon themselves, taking themselves as objects. They are able to regard and evaluate themselves, to take account of themselves and plan accordingly to bring about future states, to be self-aware or achieve consciousness with respect to their own existence. In this way, humans are a processual entity. They formulate and reflect, and this is ongoing.*

## EXPLANATION OF THE SELECTED CASE STUDIES

Chapter Four focuses on the psychological aspects of gender diaspora and social belonging. The chapter discusses theoretical approaches to gender studies and dissects the current women's movements around the world, which are modern representations of psychological diaspora, or according to this author, the feeling of being a stranger in one's homeland due to factors other than national identity (gender, sexual orientation, race, class). While traditional conceptions and theories of diaspora insist upon the importance of location and place of origin in defining diasporic communities or identities, these personal notions are important to explaining contemporary social justice movements, such as #MeToo or Black Lives Matter or Occupy. The #MeToo movement as well as other women's movements are examined in the chapter to provide an understanding of gender diaspora and mobilization via personal identity (in this case, gender).

In presenting the interviews for gender diaspora (Chapter Four), the concept of personal, or self-identity plays a major role in the women expressing their stories regarding immigration, resettlement in a Western nation, and the role of gender in diaspora politics. Personal identity theory is important to explaining the individual reasons why an individual joins a social movement or for understanding an individual's unique experiences. Personal identities as espoused by Stryker (1980, P. 60), "act as internalized positional designations" that situate individuals within a group (such as a social movement or diaspora). An ethnographic approach is taken in the case study regarding gender diaspora and the author has opted to include major portions of the interview responses in lieu of chopping them down to fit a narrative. The women that volunteered to participate shared very intimate pieces of themselves with what they could have considered the Other (a native American woman, albeit of mixed race).

The gender diaspora chapter not only features the interviews but a brief explanation of feminist studies, including intersectionality and the psychological conception of diaspora. The chapter seeks to explain the affective side of diaspora politics and gender through the voices of the Middle Eastern women interviewed, but through the lens of how academia has perceived gender politics (including diaspora) and tended to relegate women to the margins of society, even though they are most often the harbingers of culture and heritage in a host country. Although this chapter does not focus on the territorial aspects of the homeland or place of origin (as Chapter Five does) the connection to a homeland is highlighted in the responses by the interview participants.

Chapter Five makes use of secondary sources (journal articles, newspapers, academic papers, etc.) to explain contemporary diaspora politics as it relates to political territory and self-determination, focusing mainly on the struggle of the Kurds. The chapter explains traditional concepts of diaspora (emphasis on homeland and heritage), and the politics associated with modern diasporic politics, including sovereignty and international recognition. The concept of belonging to a nation and being able to identify with a specific location (and people) are key to explaining customary diaspora politics as it has been characterized by migration of a group and resettlement in a new land. Yet the Kurds have yet to garner the international recognition necessary for self-determination, particularly when it involves the divvying up of pre-established, autonomous, sovereign countries to create new ones. Diaspora politics also involve immigration politics and the admission of refugees into a host country, which has seen an increase in the wake of international terrorism and conflicts around the world (including in Syria, Myanmar, and Central Africa). Chapter Five provides great historical detail into the Kurdish situation, and juxtaposes that history with contemporary political issues facing those diasporic populations. In both Chapters Four and Five, the use of digital technologies in mobilizing participants in social movements is emphasized, as these technologies are important to connecting diasporic communities that are characterized by their transnational nature.

## REFERENCES

Blumer, H. (1936). Social Attitudes and Nonsymbolic Interaction. *Journal of Educational Sociology*, *9*(9), 515–523. doi:10.2307/2262360

Blumer, H. (1937). Social Psychology. In E. P. Schmidt (Ed.), *Man and Society: A Substantive Introduction to the Social Science*. New York: Prentice Hall.

Blumer, H. (1947). Sociological Theory in Industrial Relations. *American Sociological Review*, *12*(3), 271–278. doi:10.2307/2086516

Blumer, H. (1969). *Symbolic Interactionism: Perspective and Method.* Englewood Cliffs, NJ: Prentice-Hall.

Blumler, J. G., McLeod, J. M., & Rosengren, K. E. (1992). An Introduction to Comparative Communication Research. In J. G. Blumer, J. M. McLeod, & K. E. Rosengren (Eds.), *Comparatively Speaking: Communication and Culture Across Space and Time*. London: Sage Publishing.

Délano, A., & Gamlen, A. (2014). Comparing and Theorizing State–diaspora Relations. *Political Geography*, *41*, 43–53. doi:10.1016/j.polgeo.2014.05.005

Georgiou, M. (2002). *Diasporic Communities On-Line. A Bottom Up Experience of Transnationalism*. Journal Hommes et Migrations.

Georgiou, M. (2006). *Diaspora, Identity and the Media: Diasporic Transnationalism and Mediated Spatialities*. Cresskill, NJ: Hampton Press.

Giroux, H. (1988). *Teachers as Intellectuals: Toward a Critical Pedagogy of Learning*. Westport, CT: Greenwood Publishing Group.

Guba, E., & Lincoln, Y. (1994). Competing Paradigms in Qualitative Research. In Handbook of Qualitative Research. Thousand Oaks, CA: Sage.

Hallett, T., Shulman, D., & Fine, G. A. (2009). Peopling Organizations – The Promise of Classic Symbolic Interactionism for an Inhabited Institutionalism. In *The Oxford Handbook of Sociology and Organization Studies* (pp. 486–509). Oxford, UK: Oxford University Press.

Kissau, K., & Hunger, U. (2008). The Internet as a means of studying transnationalism and Diaspora? Paper presented at Diaspora and Transnationalism Conceptual, Theoretical and Methodological Challenges, European University Institute.

Mahoney, J. (2007). Qualitative Methodology and Comparative Politics. *Comparative Political Studies*, *40*(2), 122–144. doi:10.1177/0010414006296345

Mahoney, J., & Goertz, G. (2006). A Tale of Two Cultures: Contrasting Quantitative and Qualitative Research. *Political Analysis*, *14*(03), 227–249. doi:10.1093/pan/mpj017

Morrione, T. (2004). *Herbert George Blumer (1900-1987)*. Blackwell Encyclopedia of Sociology.

Pierson, P., & Skocpol, T. (2002). Historical Institutionalism in Contemporary Political Science. In I. Katznelson & H. V. Milner (Eds.), *Political Science: The State of the Discipline* (pp. 692–721). Washington, DC: American Political Science Association.

Pierson, P., & Skocpol, T. (2007). *The Transformation of American Politics: Activist Government and the Rise of Conservatism*. Princeton, NJ: Princeton University Press. doi:10.1515/9781400837502

Stets, J., & Burke, P. (2003). A Sociological Approach to Self and Identity. In M. Leary & J. Tangney (Eds.), *Handbook of Self and Identity*. New York: Guilford Press.

Stryker, S. (1980). *Symbolic interactionism: A social structural version*. Menlo Park, CA: Benjamin Cummings.

Wagemann, C., & Scheider, C. (2010). Qualitative Comparative Analysis (QCA) and Fuzzy-Sets: Agenda for a Research Approach and a Data Analysis Technique. *Comparative Sociology*, *9*(3), 376–396. doi:10.1163/15691321 0X12493538729838

Weber, K., & King, B. (2014). Social Movement Theory and Organization Studies. In P. Adler, P. du Gay, G. Morgan, & M. Reed (Eds.), *The Oxford Handbook of Sociology* (pp. 487–509). OUP.

# Chapter 4
# Gender Diaspora and International Women's Movements


## ABSTRACT

*This chapter outlines the psychological or affective characterizations of diaspora in relation to gender. The chapter provides a brief literature review in gender studies and diaspora, including the concept of intersectionality. The chapter discusses the #MeToo movement in terms of women feeling like strangers in their own homes (or homelands) as well as from a traditional diasporic definition features ethnographical research in the form of interviews with Middle Eastern women who inhabit the Muslim diaspora in the United States. The interviews are used to highlight real-world experiences of diaspora and the affective impact of diaspora politics, and the building of diasporic networks.*


## INTRODUCTION

*Women's and girl's bodies determine democracy: free from violence and sexual abuse, free from malnutrition and environmental degradation, free to plan families, free to not have families, free to choose their sexual lives and preferences – Zillah Eisenstein (1998, P. 161)*

DOI: 10.4018/978-1-5225-7757-7.ch004

Copyright © 2019, IGI Global. Copying or distributing in print or electronic forms without written permission of IGI Global is prohibited.

In theory there is much use of weather and natural phenomena to describe paradigm shifts in social and political realms, 'waves', 'tsunamis', 'eruptions', this author will not disappoint in carrying on with tradition in describing the seismic transition that the international community has felt since 2016. While many political theorists today will too quickly point to the election of Donald Trump as the catalyst, this abrupt change in the psychology and political calculations for women became a worldwide has been simmering under the surface, and perhaps, was brought to an outright boiling point with his election. Yet as stated, the enduring rhetoric in American politics toward women and their rights (and role) has been point of contention that has been exploited by both political parties, with one touting traditional family values, and the other, a women's right to choose her own journey. Around the world, there has been a collective (yet distinct) battle raging for increased rights for women this includes Western democracies, looked upon as the harbingers of human (thus women's) rights. These movements became more visible after the 2016 U.S. election, and arguably spread the spirit of female angst globally; movements that began as egalitarian transformed into separate calls for freedom and civil rights for women in places like Iran (2017) and Saudi Arabia (2015-present).

Social movements highlighting the plight of women have become international phenomena. Women around the world have taken a microscope to the ways in which not just the other sex treats them, but the systematic ways in which they have been relegated to the fringes of their respective societies. Women have been subjected to stereotypes about who and what they should be, can do or say, how much they deserve to be paid in relation to their male counterparts, and of course, the more obvious and gratuitous objectification and use as sexual fodder. Modern (perhaps fourth wave feminist) women's movements have popped up worldwide, and in some unlikely places, all attempting to shed light and bring about change to societies and regimes that have condoned, and at times even celebrated the inequalities between the sexes. Intersectionality has become an important concept in the study of female politics and feminism more generally. Intersectionality began to emerge in the late 1980s and is largely associated with Kimberle Crenshaw, who pointed out the exclusion of black women from the larger feminist movement by white feminists by their setting of an agenda that sought to rectify problems of the white female community (Crenshaw, 1991). Kathy Davis argues,

*While intersectionality is most often associated with US Black feminist theory and the political project of theorizing the relationships between gender, class, and race, it has also been taken up and elaborated by a second important strand within feminist theory. Feminist theorists inspired by postmodern theoretical perspectives viewed intersectionality as a welcome helpmeet in their project of deconstructing the binary oppositions and universalism inherent in the modernist paradigms of Western philosophy and science. (2008, P. 70-71)*

Thus, it became part and parcel of feminist theory and research that intersectionality or the consideration of both structural and individual (or personal) elements of the female experience by understanding political and cultural characterizations of woman-ness, as well as the individual experience of females and the impact of those political and cultural elements (Carbin & Edenheim, 2013). The ideology behind postmodernism's inclusion of intersectionality in research is perhaps best described by an editorial in *Politics and Gender*, "...Viewing gender as a stand-alone factor necessarily distorts reality. Gender never operates independently from other aspects in political life, so it is misleading to thin of gender as an autonomous category of analysis" (2007, P. 229).

This chapter highlights gender diaspora politics and the social movements that have mobilized (or morphed into) calls to rectify injustices suffered for centuries. Diaspora political theories tend to be rooted in the links and networks between peoples in their homelands versus where they have settled, mainly linked to ethnicity or religious groups. Yet there is a contemporary trend in women's studies that focuses on gender diaspora, which elaborates on the social, political, and discursive implications of diaspora by focusing on collective identity formation (emphasis on gender) and expression in the mobilization of networked social movements. Kalra, Kalhon, and Hutynuk (2005, P. 52) argue that the characterizations of diaspora (in the migration and resettlement process) may leave women "disempowered in the household for a variety of reasons, but potentially empowered in the wider society where discourses of 'rescuing' vulnerable and oppressed female members of diasporic community run rife." The women interviewed and highlighted in this chapter did express sentiments that mirror the above statement, yet all maintain that they are stronger because of their experiences as immigrants within a diaspora.

Gonzalez (2016) that beyond ethnicity, which is typically regarded as a qualifier to discuss diasporic politics traditionally, there are other characteristics such as gender that "could be used to describe the temporal state of misplacement." Noting that women are often subjected to diasporic feelings due to systemic patriarchal governance or through their personal relationships with the opposite sex. Race and ethnicity are obvious factors that emphasize difference, however, gendered identities also maintain qualitative variances in terms of how the host society views and treats gender and ethnic origin (with emphasis on gender for this work). It becomes important to examine the relationship between gender and society (both homeland and host country). Anthias (1998, P. 569) makes a compelling argument regarding postmodern (or transnational) diaspora studies, asserting, "Diaspora generally functions as a celebration of difference and the maintenance of links with ethnic and national belongingness, with roots...This tends to neglect the aspects of ethnicity that relate to boundaries of exclusion rather than boundaries constructed through identity and common experience", which would include gender, race, and ethnicity.

The international community is witnessing the migration of millions of varied populations that have been displaced by conflict, war, genocide, and in the near future, the increase in famine due to lack of natural resources (such as water, see South Africa – Day Zero). According to the United Nations 2017 International Migration Report, almost half of all international migrants are women, falling from 49 percent in 2000 to 48 percent in 2017. Yet female migrants outnumber male migrants in Europe, Northern America, Oceania, and Latin America (UN, 2017). Allison Murray asserts,

*There are now many more women involved in the largest mass migration in human history. The majority are employed on a contractual basis as foreign domestic works (the 'maid trade') in situations which often involve debts, exploitations and sexual abuse. (1998, P. 58)*

Anzaldua argues for a "mestiza consciousness" or a mode of identity that refuses static conceptions of identity and provides awareness to multiple aspects of identity (1987, P. 79). This mestiza consciousness is associated with female identity, and Anzaldua notes, "the answer to the problem between white race and the colored, between males and females, lies in healing the split that originates in the very foundation of our lives, our culture, our languages, our thoughts" (1987, P. 102). Anthias critiqued diaspora scholars for using concrete notions such as "origin" and "true belonging", which she argued did not provide adequate attention to problems such as divisions within ethnic communities or transcultural issues. She noted,

*...the lack of attention given to transethnic solidarities, such as those against racism, of class, of gender, of social movements, is deeply worrying from the perspective of the development of multiculturality, and more inclusive notions of belonging. For a discourse of antiracism and social mobilization of a transethnic (as opposed to a transnational) character, cannot be easily accommodated, within the discourse of the diaspora, where it retains its dependence on 'homeland' and 'origin', however configured. (1987, P. 102)*

The psychological aspect of diaspora has been explored by theorists such as Kristeva, who argues in *Strangers to Ourselves,* that the foreigner "lives within us: he is the hidden face of our identity, the space that wrecks our abode, the time in which understanding and affinity founder. By recognizing him within ourselves, we are spared detesting him in himself...The foreigner comes in when the consciousness of my difference arises, and he disappears when we all acknowledge ourselves as foreigners, unamenable to bonds and communities (1991, P. 1). Gonzalez concludes that too often research on diaspora is focused on broader migration of peoples or statelessness, but it can be as personal as one's gender "separat[ing] them from their community/ life and forc[ing] them into a world of confusion and misrepresentation" (2016). This sentiment was expressed by a majority of the women that were interviewed for this work and will be dissected later in this chapter. They expressed not just feelings of exclusion in a new place (the U.S.), but also as Muslim women, also expressed the sadness felt by watching their children grow up without many of the customs and cultural traditions that they themselves experienced as young women living in the Middle East. Nititham notes,

*Members of minority ethnic communities live in racial and ethnic constructions as well as among borders of existence, such as renewing their immigration status, possibly living isolated from friends and/or family, not belonging 'here' or 'there' or one particular place. Policies which impede full access to privileges accorded to citizens solidify these borders, as well as homogenizing the marginalized. (2008, P. 76)*

The women interviewed for this chapter expressed a deep sadness at what was perceived to be a lack of belonging, both when they returned to their homeland on visits, and in their place of resettlement (Dallas, Texas). It was nearly unanimously expressed that raising children in the host country could be disheartening and disorienting when attempting to maintain and inject traditional (homeland) culture and norms into children positioned between cultures (transcultural). El-Tayeb (2012, P. 91) notes that European states in the face of global terrorism, have placed a category on Muslim women and racialize these women, projecting stereotypes and gender assumptions upon them. She goes on to assert, "The framing of the inability to belong as an individual/cultural failure rather than as the outcome of structural and discursive exclusions works to disempower and alienate groups who threaten the identifications on which Europeanness continues to be built" (2012, P. 91). Puar describes the victimization that diasporic women can face, noting the persecution of women,

*This time [was] not only of her oppressive, patriarchal, backward culture and 'extended' family but also of her supposed longings to assimilate into white society and the racism she faces within it. She is seen to crave all that the West has to offer, but according to dominant white gazes, her culture holds her back, and only the 'rebels' succeed. (1995, P. 25)*

The question of diasporic resistance to host society/culture, the population is having to navigate the traditions of their homeland and belonging in a new society, both through the role of being a woman and a minority. Often women are protective of cultural traditions, particularly, if they are condemned (or at least looked upon as strange) by the host population (e.g. female genital mutilation; call to prayers, etc.). Anthias and Yuval Davis (1989) assert that women are reproducers of ethnic and national ideologies and play a central role in the transmission of cultural values and norms. Women who are viewed as challenging the norms of their heritage are often met with criticism of becoming *westernized*, and trading their culture in for a more societally appropriate conception. Thiara notes,

*Women have often been seen as damaging the interests of the ethnic groups because they engage in an internal critique that is seen to be detrimental to the group project, as reflected in the promulgation of leaders that violence against women is not a problem...Moreover, discussions about ethnic mobilization always focuses on benefiting the group, rather than also contesting and attempting to transform inequalities within as well as without. (2003, P. 142)*

Hua (2011) argues that citizenship is a "deeply gendered" concept and has been presented over the course of history in the literature as "male citizen with his interests and concerns dictating the agenda" (P. 46). Numerous theories on citizenship note that it is a bidirectional process that involves a government placing obligations on a citizen (e.g. paying taxes, serving in the military) and protecting certain rights. In both obligations Hua would argue that citizenship, thus is intrinsically linked to male-ness, in many societies around the world (throughout their development and in some places, now) women are not able to work and thus cannot pay taxes on their own. By linking citizenship to fighting and potentially dying for one's country as a way to prove loyalty, citizenship is again (arguably) linked to the male – as a majority of military members around the world today are still men. Pettman (1999, P. 207) argues that citizenship does tend to be centered on the male, and "rests in ambiguous ways on the private support world of family, home and women". As Wendy Brown notes in regards to the construction of gender (and arguably citizenship), "There is not as Judith Butler recently remarked first gender and then the apparatus that regulates it; gender does not exist prior to its regulation" (2005, P. 123). The state, which traditionally boasts a patriarchal hierarchy, is often the entity that is regulating the genders (at least politically and economically), and society often reaffirms whatever ideals regarding gender (equality, liberty, loyalty) are first established by the state (and its officials who give cues as to how people within a civil society should be treated).

Nyla Khan asserts, "Writers create a site on which local thought-patterns, structures, and rhythms are accompanied by the delineation of an alternative social reality. Their writings not only coin neologisms, but also incorporate indigenous languages and dialects that are signifiers of the local as opposed to the universal." It is the sustained opposition between two discursive systems that prevents the transnational from conforming to a stringent system of representation. She argues these discursive moments are important in the creation and maintenance of diaspora, and notes,

*In the 1950s and 1960s, South Asian writers in English attempted to affiliate South Asian writing with the dominant forms of the English novel. The generation of V. S. Naipaul and Anita Desai did not make a serious endeavor to either explore indigenous narrative forms or to appropriate the English language to the South Asian context. In these writings, the social, cultural, and political realms are often places of disillusionment and enable the analysis of individual aberrations. (2018, personal correspondence)*

During the 1980s, South Asian writing in English experienced a revival, with a new generation of writers challenging the idea of national unity and integrity of the nation-state. These writers attempted to explain the history of the nationalist struggle in a form that negates colonialism. Thus the resulting works incorporate "memory, imagination, and folk-tale into sanctioned versions of history and is skeptical about the stability of the nation and its symbols" (Khan, 2018). As Mee observes about this generation of Indian novelists, "It has been deployed to call the globalization of culture to local account, to foreground the difficulties of translation and the possibilities of dialogue" (2011, P. 336). Following the same logic, Mohanty (2003) makes an argument against the distinction between *East* and *West*, *Western* and *Non-Western*, as well as *North* and *South* in analyzing differences in gender politics in the post-globalized world. She notes, "Perhaps it is no longer simply an issue of Western eyes, but rather how the West is inside and continually reconfigures globally, racially, and in terms of gender. Without this recognition, a necessary link between feminist scholarship/analytic frames and organizing/activist projects is impossible" (Mohanty, 2003, P. 515). However, celebration of dislocation as the contentious site where psychological and spiritual emancipation might be achieved, like universalizing the detached position of an exile, has been attacked for its lack of affiliation with local politics in South Asia. Khan concludes,

*Nationalist discourse in South Asia creates the dichotomy of the inner/outer in order to make the sanctity of the inviolable inner domain look traditional. Nationalist writers assert that as long as the inner or spiritual distinctiveness of the culture is retained, a postcolonial nation can make the required adjustments to cope with a modern material world without losing its essential identity. The result, however, is not the orderly process of modernization but rather the continued immiseration of women. (2018, personal correspondence)*

Authors and their works have shed awareness on varied diasporas throughout the world and history, often pushing the boundaries of what the audience perceives to be innovative in the field of political/social science, and particularly in gender studies (with an emphasis on the female diasporic experience). Mohanty (2003) dissects the feminist solidarity or comparative feminist studies model for analyzing gender politics. This framework conceives of local and global (speaking of physical boundaries/territory) as existing simultaneously and in conjunction. Thus, the model emphasizes the "links, the relationships, between the local and the global that are foregrounded, and these links are conceptual, material, temporal, contextual, and so on (Mohanty, 2003, P. 521). For example, an examination of the history and politicization of hijab in relation to the aesthetic gendering of the Muslim woman diaspora and how women across the world can relate to similar discrimination they have faced for choosing to wear a symbol of their faith and modesty. The politicization of hijab began during the independence movements in the 1950s, when it became a symbol for isolation and subjugation for Islamists and for the majority of working-class women it was a symbol of defiance to colonialism and westernization. Ahmed argues,

*The hijab attests to the fact that, at least as regards the Islamic world, the discourses of resistance and rejection are inextricably informed by the languages and ideas developed and disseminated by the West to no less degree than are the languages of those openly advocating emulation of the West. (1992, P. 235)*

The comparative model provides for a more comprehensive view of the differences and similarities that exist regarding women from diverse areas of the world, particularly in relation to diaspora. According to Pinto (2013, P. 4), "In bringing the full weight of diaspora to bear on what and how we read for the intersections of difference, these innovative new texts insist on the incommensurability of various registers of identity.... Literary and cultural production are intimately and pervasively present in how we construct analytics of race, gender, and location." The diversified nature of identity in the transnational world becomes another intersectional moment for academic research, as subfields of comparative politics (which would be an important field of inquiry for diaspora studies) such as gender and queer studies emerge and again question how diasporic communities are formed. Contemporary diasporas challenge the historically accepted manners of acquiring knowledge about one's heritage, homeland, culture, and identity. According to Pinto (2013, P. 7), "Diaspora...challenge the order of things – the way we come to recognize and interpret our specific historical and social realties – in its difficult play between the known and the unknown, between recognizable forms of being, knowing, belonging, and acting in the world and the new forms that emerge as we try to understand its shifts."

Modern theories of diaspora attempt to find the commonalities in analysis and explanation between diaspora and feminist (gender) studies, Pinto (2013) notes this first begins by reconsidering the importance of location. Pinto notes, "...Cultural flows are just as salient markers of "diaspora" as the migration of peoples, it tracks iconographies, art objects, and ideologies to create new networks of diaspora possibility beyond historically and geographically corresponding subjects" (2013, P. 11).

## GENDER DIASPORA IN THE UNITED STATES

Khan notes the disconnection of the essential identity of women in diasporic communities, and while her research tends to focus on Indian and South Asian women, it is a sentiment that was expressed via interviews with members of the Muslim diasporic community in the United States (more specifically, Dallas, Texas). The author interviewed six women currently living in Dallas identified with the help of the Council on American-Islamic Relations (CAIR) who immigrated to the United States for various reasons. The author sought to understand how and why these women immigrated, their gender roles and differentiation among societies (host and homeland), and their attachment to culture, traditions, and heritage that they left behind in their places of origin. The women spanned in age from early thirties to late forties, and hailed from countries of conflict (historically and currently), including Syria and Palestine. The author presented each interview participant with a disclosure agreement, informing them of their rights to information and a description of use of the research collected from the interviews, in accordance with ethical standards. The interviewees were able to opt-out of using their real names in effort to protect themselves and families from reprisal. The interviews were recorded via an iPhone and the author took detailed documentation of the meeting as well. Parts of the interviews were mournful, the author will admit to becoming teary on more than one occasion while listening to the sometimes tragic sentiments of everyday women attempting to navigate a new world with courage. What follows is a narrative, detailed account of the six women and their experience of diaspora and host country politics, which should shed a more personal light on the psychological impact of diaspora on women and family.

The interviews presented were conducted on May 23 (one phone interview) and May 24, 2018 (in-person) with the assistance of the Council on American-Islamic Relations (CAIR) in Dallas, Texas. The council was established in 1994 and advocates on behalf of Muslims and civil liberties, which has assisted in the establishment of the Muslim diasporic community within the United States. The council works as a network for Muslim-Americans and Muslims living in America, making sure that the voice of these groups is not marginalized in American politics and society. The organization has a national office headquartered in Washington D.C., as well as regional offices in many states across the U.S., which assist in providing awareness and promote understanding in state and local politics, including Oklahoma and Kansas. CAIR is an important network foundation for social and political activism, which the council also assists in fomenting, according to the CAIR website, the group "seeks to empower the American Muslim community and encourage their participation in political and social activism." The 2018 Executive Report from CAIR notes "an increase in the onslaught of institutional and individual prejudice against American Muslims in 2017" (CAIR, 2018, P. 5), and the research contained in the document includes an overview of how the Muslim community in America are pushing back against the new wave of anti-Other rhetoric in American political society. "Where CAIR is present, the local community is more likely to report cases (of discrimination, harassment, bullying, vandalism) to the organization. Thus, in states like California and Florida where CAIR has multiple offices, a higher number of cases are expected than in states like Tennessee and Montana where the organization does not have offices" (CAIR, 2018, P. 9). The author believed it crucial to coordinate the interviews with an organization that was trusted within the diasporic community such as CAIR, as it provided legitimacy to the fact that the author would use the words of the community to best highlight the experiences of the women.

The participants volunteered their time for no compensation and were told what the nature and subject of the conversation would be, without divulging too much information on specific questions that may have stunted their ability to emote in the group environment. Each participant signed a consent form to participate and able to designate whether or not they used their real name in the work itself. The author took great care to ask questions of the women that did not make them feel uncomfortable, yet were intimate enough to get an true understanding of what it feels to not belong (or perceive of that) in the society that one inhabits. The author consciously chose to conduct the interviews of the women at the same time, or a group interview, to allow the women (who all knew or know of each other due to their proximity and involvement in the diasporic community) to realize that they were not alone in their feelings of *homelessness* (in the sense that one does not feel at home in their place of origin, nor in the place they have chosen to live). There is a conflict of wanting to return to the place of origin yet not wanting to abandon the newfound security or improved living conditions (politically, economically, socially), Demmers argues that this produces a "fear of peace" within diasporic communities as the prospect of peace in the homeland removes "moral justification(s) to live abroad" (2007, P. 15). Hall underscores the necessity of this yearning for a homeland in maintaining diasporic identity, noting, "Although you can never go back to the past, you do have a sense of loss of an intimate connection with a history, a landscape, family, tradition, custom – the vernacular. In a sense, this is the fate of all modern people – we have to lose those connections, but we seem to require the myth, the illusion that we are going to go back to them (1990, P. 349–350). The sense of longing to belong to the host society and yet yearning to return to the homeland was expressed by at least two of the participants. As Baser and Swain assert,

*The notion of a 'secure homeland', a place to return in time, plays a very important role in diaspora behavior, yet it has been proven by various cases that diaspora members are reluctant to leave the hostland when it comes to returning home if their goals are somehow achieved. (2009, P. 49)*

The interviews will be presented in a question-answer format, the author will make sure to differentiate between the voices of the women, as they have different ethnic backgrounds that are unique to their experiences of migration and diaspora. The six women represent Palestine/Jordan, Syria (two participants originated in Syria), Egypt, Pakistan, and Turkey; the women will be referred to by their place of origin as way to simplify the responses. The author initiated the discussion by asking a question of origin, asking them to narrate their immigration experience, what caused the migration, and if they experienced any hardships in the journey.

**Palestine/Jordan***: I received a Masters [degree] in Edinburgh in 2009, and taught in Jordan. I was able to come to the University of North Texas, teaching English as Second Language; while at the university, I applied for the doctoral program and was approved. But I returned to Jordan and postponed my attendance until August 2010 when I returned to the United States and completed my Ph.D. in 2015. During 2014, I met the man who would become my husband, but I went back to Jordan to take a tenured position at Jordan University. My husband came to Jordan, converted his religion, and we moved back to the U.S. in August 2016. I believed that assimilation would* *be better (easier) in U.S. rather than Jordan. After marrying a foreigner, an American, but not just an American, a fourth generation Japanese-American, I never thought it would happen. My family is Palestinian, we moved to Jordan after the Six Days War, I was born in Jordan. I consider myself to be both Jordan-Palestinian/Palestinian-Jordanian. I tend not to go by the place a person was born, as I feel an attachment to places where parents came from, even though I was not born there. In U.S., you are American first, in Middle East, we are attached to places where the family comes from. I had no hardships and was lucky enough to be approved for my Ph.D. but there were no scholarship for immigrants available, which could have impeded my ability to complete a doctorate. I was able to schedule a meeting with chair of my department, who calls director of a division, and they got me a teaching position fellowship, which qualified me for in-state tuition and a small salary. Besides being away from the family, I have had a wonderful experience in the U.S., I have a family at UNT. I consider them my first family in America. This is my real home here.*

**Pakistan:** *My husband received a medical degree in Pakistan and his training brought us to the U.S., first to Michigan and finally to Texas. It was difficult for the first year, with my husband being quite busy in his medical program, I had a large extended family to rely on in the U.S., but felt less independent than I did in Pakistan.*

**Turkey:** *I met my husband online, he was in Philadelphia working at a children's hospital, and I was in Turkey. We married in Turkey and moved to the United States in 2000, I lived in Brooklyn during the September 11, 2001 attacks, and have lived in Georgia as well before settling in Texas. I felt the effect of Islamaphobia [after September 11th] even though I was not a practicing Muslim at the time, it was the stigma attached to the Muslim community afterwards that impacted me.*

**Syria 1:** *I was engaged in Syria and we decided to come to the United States as students, which was not easy. I had trouble doing mundane activities [such as grocery shopping] because I looked different than other people. At first I was excited to break free of Syria, but after living in the U.S. for 18 years and having three children in America, I am finding myself losing my Arabic identity.*

**Egypt:** *I met my husband in Egypt. He came to the United States in 1995 to study medicine and stayed, but upon visiting family in Egypt we met as he was looking for a bride. I was not considering moving to the United States before meeting him. The first time I left Egypt, I realized that I was now alone in a new place, upon moving to the U.S. I quickly developed depression and starting gaining weight. We lived in Las Vegas for 14 years, and during that time [post-September 11th] I was covered in hijab while living my daily life, and was largely unmolested, I recall only three times that I was approached, in one case was accused of hating Jesus. I live an Islamic lifestyle in the United States, but I long for my country. I visit typically once a year.*

**Syria 2:** *I was married at age 19, in the year 2000, and moved the United States afterwards. My husband's family was already settled in the U.S., which assisted with my resettling. I went back to college for one year for English, but was unable to finish my degree due to having children. I feel like I cannot go back [to Syria], it has been 8 years.*

The second question deals with the political aspects in the women's countries of origin and how the politics of that country may be inhibiting the return of diasporic populations to their homelands. Most of the women (themselves) expressed a fundamental lack of awareness of their homeland politics, or simply were apathetic about it. However, there are some notable standout responses below, including the Egyptian and Palestinian/Jordanian women. The second question to the interviewees is as follows: Describe the politics in your home country.

**Palestine/Jordan:** *In terms of Palestine, I am not happy with what is going on there, involving the PLA [Palestine Liberation Army], but I don't see myself as qualified to judge. In general, the division in Gaza/West Bank, and moving of the embassy to Jerusalem, there seems to be a passive attitude of politicians [both in the West and Middle East]. I am upset and angry. For the [Palestinian] people, we always feel sorry for these people, running to their death and giving [Israel] an excuse to attack by coming to the border. But at the end of the day, when thinking of them, I think of a person in prison for life: what are their options? [They] choose the way that we [they] are going to die. [They are] Choosing to die for a purpose, and to be free from the politics at the end in of their lives. There is an imbalanced point of view among Western media in regards to Israelis and Muslims, [or] West versus East. There is much misrepresentation, and I think that Muslims are to be* *blamed for that, we provide a voice to the Other to talk about us; even our political leaders do not speak for us. This was highlighted with the failure of Arab Spring [she was discussing Egypt], even our leaders are not with us. I don't blame the West, I blame Arabs and the Middle East, there is no channel between the people and the leaders! [She becomes emphatic here - exclamation point added by author for emphasis]. We [East/West] don't speak the same the language and are not coming from same background, don't blame others for taking advantage of you. Before media perception can change we [Muslims] have to change the attitude about ourselves; improve the image of ourselves first. We must fix the internal image, fix our own house and then look at relations with the West.*

**Pakistan:** *There is a power struggle in Pakistan, and corruption is deeply embedded [within the political system]. I feel there is no hope of improvement without educating the younger generation. Religious political parties and leaders have distorted the religion in order to maintain legitimacy. Starting at the individual level, Pakistani citizens must be educated.*

**Turkey:** *I feel that Erdogan leads well; he is standing up for Palestine. There are many against him [see the 2016 political coup that sought to install a new regime], but I do not see him as a dictator. Everyone is free in Turkey, there is not pressure to be Islamic; but Western media presents [the regime] as [an] evil infrastructure.*

**Syria 1:** *The Arab Spring made me hopeful that conditions could improve quickly [initially]. [Before the movements] Syria was always calm and settled – I wish now that the Arab Spring did not happen anywhere. Change needs to occur from within the country, but it is too late now, the situation feels hopeless. Assad has been put in a bad position [arguably by coalition forces fighting the Islamic State at the same time the regime is fighting opposition forces that seek to destabilize Assad's rule]. I would like to, if things get better, to go home and rebuild, but my child [raised in America] says, 'let them take care of themselves'.*

**Egypt:** *The government [are] hypocritical in the region. The 1952 "revolution" [used air quotes to denote sarcasm] was a coup, the military took power (Nassar) and then the introduction of Sadat who was generally loved in Egypt and tried to bring about peace, but was murdered. Enter Mubarak and his linage of corruption, who had to be taught and then glued himself to the* *presidential chair due to a change in the constitution. The fake Arab Spring ensues and he leaves after 18 days because the corruption was unbelievable. [She calls the Arab Spring in Egypt fake because the people united for change not the installation of a military regime]. Now al-Sisi is in power and is aligned with Israel. Under al-Sisi women are treated badly, the country has lost the concept of having educated women.*

**Syria 2:** *[The woman mirrors what the first Syrian woman stated, but goes onto note] Kids are worse now because they are being indoctrinated.*

The following narrative combines multiple questions regarding gender and diaspora including: Describe the status and role of women in your homeland. What does it mean/entail to be a woman?; How has your personal experience changed since you have been in the United States?; Do you feel part of a collective within the American society or do you feel like an outsider, or Other?; and What is your opinion of the international women's movements (e.g.: Iran/India/U.S.)?

**Palestine/Jordan:** *My mom and father did not finish high school, they were married in Jordan, and my mom was separated from her family during war. After marriage they moved to Kuwait for months. I was brought up both parents in love with each other and dedicated to family and children needs. Completing our education was the priority for the family - for both sexes. My mother was an educated person but in charge of the household, which was regimented. My father traveled a lot, so responsibility was in my mom's hands. There are some changes [between home and host country roles]. I have four sisters, of which I am the oldest, all of us are married, all of us have finished Bachelors degrees, some of us work and some don't, but all are in charge of their families. It does not matter where you are Dubai, Jordan, the United States; we take care of our children, homework, cleaning, groceries; we all have the same responsibilities. Even if they are not working for an income, there is power from bringing up the kids it is still doing something regardless of personal income. Women in the Middle East are doing the same things as any woman here; and those working still have same responsibilities. Perhaps Middle Eastern women here are more powerful by finishing their education and sometimes being married to right person (wealthy); but they do the same things that upper class white women do. [In regards to the international women's movements] Things are changing but in Jordan* *women are still powerless. It depends on social class, but there are problems with mixing religion and law, so many women do not understand their rights from an Islamic point of view and the law in general, mixing religion with right and wrong. I do not like to look at a movement as international; each society has its own issues and problems to deal with. We [women] share the same problems of harassment, assault, and rape, but each society has its own condition. I don't mind exposing my society or any patriarchal society, as long as I am exposing it for change. In Jordan, Palestine, the U.S. at this point there is another agenda – this is personal agenda in order to find a space for me in this society or personal achievement – but when I fight with my sisters in Jordan, I am doing it to be with them and challenge the system. [Regarding diasporic sentiment] Sure, I experience Othering, at concerts here in Irving, Texas, for example, older, white people coming to classical concerts look at the 'hijabi' and seem to question whether I like music. When I approach, they will move, but I believe in self-confidence. I am not doing anything wrong by wearing my hijab or by covering my body or coming to a concert – you are only defending something that is wrong – it is not wrong. The women's movement is about doing what you want with your body – I have that same right to cover my body [as another woman does to show hers] it does not mean I cannot assimilate. I will be in control of my assimilation to be able to function. I am married to an American husband, he can meet me in the middle of the road, but cannot walk all the way – if I want them to accept me, I must alter but not change – keep my essential Arab identity, but not change. I have never been attacked, but do experience problems with students every other semester. I am a foreigner teaching them their language, and whether I'm qualified or not does not matter, whether I look like a Muslim or not is what does to some. They can choose to accept me or choose another instructor. America is my home. When I'm driving, I have some moments to think about whether it is my home. I have become familiar with places and feel an attachment that I want to resist sometimes. It took time to accept being here or there; but after so many years, why not? I must think about it as home. I went to Jordan last year and felt as if it was not my home anymore. I am in control of my life in Jordan and in America. To be honest, when they [my family] come to United States I do not believe it will add something to them or make them. If you are not successful or established or cultured this country will not add to you; it will take from you as much as it will give. You must know what you offer and what you can get.*

**Pakistan:** *There is a large spectrum of perceptions of women, for instance many American woman thought as a Middle Eastern woman, I was uneducated. I was raised one of four sister and was taught that we all must have higher education degrees and earn our own way. I was trained to be independent and follow my talent. [On international women's movements] I do not see the movements coming together. Women have not found strong connections with each other and view each other as oddities. It is not beneficial to unite [in terms of East/West movements], we must focus on the local aspects of change and decide for ourselves. [On diaspora] I have experienced inner growth psychologically; I do not identify as solely Pakistani. Being Pakistani is important but being Muslim is number one for me. I have found like-minded people that have roots, which grounds me. I have started participating more within the American system, voting [she divulged that she voted for Hillary Clinton, but her husband did not]. This is also my home, and I have become part of the fabric [of the community], but at the same time, I will not be accepted fully by that community.*

**Turkey:** *I was raised in a liberal family that attained higher education, but was also taught that it is most important to have a family, kids. [On diaspora] I have mixed feelings [regarding my home], I visit Turkey each year, but when I am in Turkey more than a month, I miss the U.S. My children are more American than Turkish. I do not feel like people accept me [in the U.S.], I feel like I belong but knowing I won't be accepted bothers me. I long for the feeling that I belong somewhere.*

**Syria 1:** *I come from a more traditional family. Females are not expected to work as fathers and brothers are to provide for the women. Women in Syria are now being educated, which is positive. I felt I needed to be more independent than my mother. American women are so independent because society forces them to be; they take on too much for themselves and American men look to the woman to do it all. It should be fifty-fifty. [On diaspora] I do not belong either here or there. I feel like a stranger in Syria because I am viewed differently, there is not the same acceptance of diversity. I felt like an outsider a lot, but I did it to myself, I isolated myself, believing I would never be fully American. I needed to find myself. I decided that if you want to make it, you can; people will accept you, it is in your hands, you must be strong, be active, do not wait for them.*

**Egypt:** *Women are not educated in the villages, but they are strong and take on a lot of responsibility. The men work and do not do anything when at home; the [American] woman is having to work and take on everything. When I came to the United States, I was able to be independent. The U.S. says women are equal and yet they are not ready for Hillary [Clinton], there is a subtle misogyny here as well. [On Diaspora] The problems within the Muslim community in America started around September 11, 2001, after the event I realized that I did not have a single American friend. Hatred was here and the media painted Muslims as the enemy of the American people [which arguably placed a strain on the diasporic community and its relationship with the host country, and subsequent politics]. I was wary of participating in our [she placed great emphasis on the fact that she felt that the United States is her home – italics added by author to display that sentiment]. I fear for my kids, who truly do feel like America is their home, particularly Dallas. I belong in the American society but within the Muslim community, I do not think I will ever belong entirely. I want to contribute to my society and stay safe.*

As is evident in the responses above, the Muslim diasporic community within the United States exists and is fairly active in contemporary American politics, with organizations like CAIR and the Southern Law Poverty Center assisting in advocating for the rights of Muslims and other groups that face racial, religious, or ethnic discrimination. These women both feel as if they individually fit within the American society and yet simultaneously feel it is impossible to conceive of ever truly belonging to the fabric of America wholly. There is still a strong connection to the homeland that is evident with all of the women, and yet a longing to not be perceived as the Other within the host country. Arguably the politics of the day can make the feeling of Otherness more palpable than it may have been before the election of a nationalist president, but many of the participants noted a shift among the American populace in conjunction with the attacks of September 11, 2001. The danger in alienating and Othering the Muslim diasporic community is one of national security for the United States, it is critical that the lines of communication and trust remain open between the government, civil society, and diasporic community in order for the entities to work together on issues of domestic terrorism or identifying rogue actors within the community. As Stacey (2017) argues, it behooves the U.S. government to not vilify the Muslim-American community but to utilize their resources and knowledge of their community to protect the nation from lone wolf and other domestic terrorist attacks.

While there have been multiple movements and organizations established to provide awareness to the lack of women's (and human) rights around the world, there has been a void between policy and norm setting at the governmental level, perhaps because some elected officials may be concerned how the #MeToo movement may impact their careers and lives (e.g., Trump). The characteristic of gender and equal rights has also historically met confusion and complication in achieving goals when dealing with non-state actors, such as the church and/or the civil society of the country, which may be adverse to reforming gender roles. Even within social movement organizations (or lack thereof) as in the U.S. Occupy Movement that certainly included women in its membership, but failed to focus its message or ideology on one that emphasized increased rights for the marginalized beyond class and wealth status. Occupy amalgamated its participants into a movement that focused on economic inequality from a purely economic standpoint, the movement ideology did not dive into further (and more nuanced) contributing factors to this vast inequality that exists in the United States, such as race and gender, leaving the movement open to be conveyed in the media and to the populace as a leaderless protest movement of predominately white men. Occupy failed to diversify its message and lost a significant opportunity to frame the question of inequality in America as systemic for some and not for others, and to address those inequities. Bhattacharjya et al. (2013, P. 288) argue, "All social movements, including women's movements, need to commit to a holistic approach to inequality, recognizing identities based on gender, ethnicity, caste, age, class, sexual orientation, and (dis)ability, and championing arguments and actions that respond to the human rights demands of everyone." This provides a bridge back to diaspora. It has been argued that in terms of gender, diaspora studies tend to focus on the struggle of women over that of men – this work adds to the literature on gender diaspora from a psychological (and sentimental) perspective, which very often can act as catalysts to participation in dissent.

Theorists on feminism, such as Moallem (2006) argue that to better understand the intersection of national identity and gender politics that a "modernist feminist internationalist agenda" must be established, which is problematic for many of the reasons pointed out by the interview participants. Particularly troubling is the assumption that local and global politics (or the struggle of women in various political systems) can be approached in a unified manner, instead of highlighting the differences between the countries and the cultures being examined. Davies and Bansal (2010) note that many new social movements are attempting to detach from local and historical foundations (heritage/tradition) and reattach to more global understandings – in doing so there is a leveling of difference among societies, politics, and human rights. Feminist scholar Chandra Mohanty (2003) defends her groundbreaking work Under Western Eyes (1986), in which she calls on feminist studies to engage more with the women (groups) being examined on an individual level. She argues, "My insistence on the specificity of difference is based on a vision of equality attentive to power differences within and among the various communities of women" (Mohanty, 2003, P. 502). This author adheres to this sentiment with all forms of research, not just gender studies.

As the following chapter will note, it is necessary to dissect instances of collective action (diasporic or not) at an individual level, this author does so employing historical institutionalism (as discussed in Chapter Three). This approach provides social, political, cultural, and economic understanding of the peoples being analyzed and the history of the present sociopolitical situation. The following chapter examines the political conception of diaspora with emphasis on the acquisition and protection of sovereign national borders and a national identity. The chapter highlights a salient case of contemporary diasporic political movements for self-determination, the Kurdish people.

## REFERENCES

Ahmed, L. (1992). *Women and Gender in Islam: Historical Roots of a Modern Debate*. Yale University Press.

Anthias, F. (1998). Evaluating Diaspora: Beyond Ethnicity? *Sociology*, *32*(3), 557–580.

Anthias, F., & Yuval-Davis, N. (1989). *Woman-Nation-State*. London: Macmillan.

Anzaldua, G. (1987). *Borderlands/La Frontera: The New Mestiza*. Aunt Lute Books.

Baser, B., & Swain, A. (2009). Diaspora Design Versus Homeland Realities: Case Study of Armenian Diaspora. *Caucasian Review of International Affairs*, *3*(1), 45–62.

Beckwith, K., & Baldez, L. (2007). From the Editors. *Politics & Gender, 3*(1), 1–5. doi:10.1017/S1743923X07070018

Bhattacharjya, M., Birchall, J., Caro, P., Kelleher, D., & Sahasranaman, V. (2013). Why gender matters in activism: Feminism and social justice movements. *Gender and Development, 21*(2), 277–293. doi:10.1080/13552074.2013.802150

Brown, W. (2005). *Edgework: Essays on Knowledge and Politics*. Princeton University Press.

Carbin, M., & Edenheim, S. (2013). The intersectional turn in feminist theory: A dream of a common language? *European Journal of Women's Studies, 20*(3), 233–248. doi:10.1177/1350506813484723

Council on American-Islamic Relations. (2018). *CAIR Civil Rights Report 2017*. Accessed from: https://www.cairoklahoma.com/resource/targeted/

Crenshaw, K. (1991). Mapping the Margins: Intersectionality, Identity Politics, and Violence against Women of Color. *Stanford Law Review, 43*(6), 1241–1299. doi:10.2307/1229039

Davis, K. (2008). Intersectionality as buzzword: A sociology of science perspective on what makes a feminist theory successful. *Feminist Theory, 9*(1), 67–85. doi:10.1177/1464700108086364

Eisenstein, Z. (1998). *Global Obscenities: Patriarchy, Capitalism, and the Lure of Cyberfantasy*. New York: New York University Press.

El-Tayeb, F. (2012). *European Others: Queering Ethnicity in Post-National Europe*. Minneapolis: University of Minnesota.

Gonzalez, R. (2016). *Gender Diaspora: Reclaiming the Sex. Diaspora and Identity*. Accessed from: https://medium.com/diaspora-identity/gender-diaspora-reclaiming-the-sex-848bbbe513f5

Hall, S. (1990). Cultural identity and diaspora. In J. Rutherford (Ed.), *Identity: Community, Culture, Difference* (pp. 222–237). London: Lawrence & Wishart.

Hua, A. (2011). Homing Desire, Cultural Citizenship, and Diasporic Imaginings. *Journal of International Women's Studies, 12*(4), 45–56.

Kalra, V., Kalhon, R., & Hutynuk. (2005). *Diaspora and Hybridity*. London: Sage Publications.

Kristeva, J. (1991). *Strangers to Ourselves*. New York: Columbia University Press.

Mee, J. (2011). *Conversable Worlds: Literature, Contention, and Community 1762 to 1830*. Oxford, UK: Oxford University Press. doi:10.1093/acprof:oso/9780199591749.001.0001

Moallem, M., Freedman, E., Narayan, U., Harding, S., Mohanty, C., & Wing, A. K. (2006). Feminist Scholarship and the Internationalization of Women's Studies. *Feminist Studies*, *32*(2), 332–531. doi:10.2307/20459089

Mohanty, C. (2003). "Under Western Eyes" Revisited: Feminist Solidarity through Anticapitalist Struggles. *Signs (Chicago, Ill.)*, *28*(2), 499–535. doi:10.1086/342914

Murray, A. (1998). Debt Bondage and Trafficking: Don't Believe the Hype. Global Sex Workers, 51-64.

Nititham, D. S. (2008). Locating the self in diaspora space. *Translocations: The Irish Migration, Race and Social Transformation Review*, *3*(1), 1–17.

Pettman, J. J. (1999). Globalisation and the Gendered Politics of Citizenship. In N. Y. Davis & P. Werbner (Eds.), *Women, Citizenship and Difference*. London: Zed Books.

Pinto, S. (2013). *Difficult Diasporas: The Transnational Feminist Aesthetic of the Black Atlantic*. New York: New York University Press. doi:10.18574/nyu/9780814759486.001.0001

Puar, J. (1995). Resituating Discourses of "Whiteness" and "Asianness" in Northern England: Second Generation Sikh Women and Constructions of Identity. *Socialist Review*, *24*(1/2), 21–53.

Stacey, E. (2017). *Combatting Internet-Enabled Terrorism: Emerging Research and Opportunities*. IGI Global. doi:10.4018/978-1-5225-2190-7

Thiara, R. (2003). South Asian Women and Collective Action in Britain. In J. Andall (Ed.), *Gender and Ethnicity in Contemporary Europe*. Oxford, UK: Berg.

United Nations. (2017). *International Migration Report*. Retrieved from http://www.un.org/en/development/desa/population/migration/publications/migrationreport/docs/MigrationReport2017_Highlights.pdf

# Chapter 5
# Territorial Diaspora Politics:
## Peoples and Lands


## ABSTRACT

*This chapter focuses on the classical or traditional definition of diaspora as it relates to a place of origin and/or an attachment to a homeland (whether real or perceived). The chapter highlights theories of classical diaspora and provides an in-depth analysis into the contemporary Kurdish situation of statelessness and increased claims to land (due to their involvement with the fight against the Islamic State). The chapter also makes brief mention of the other prominent case of contemporary diaspora politics in the Middle East, that of the Palestinians. The chapter explains the struggle of the Kurds to self-determination and to establish an autonomous state, and highlights the adoption and use of digital technologies by diasporic communities, which allows for the facilitation of diasporic communities and networks that transcend traditional borders.*


## INTRODUCTION

Traditional concepts of diaspora maintain the importance of place of origin and migration as roots of political and social condition. Migration politics have become a fairly recent but critical piece of national law and homeland security policy. Gamlen et al. (2013) note that more than half of United Nations member nations have dedicated bureaucratic entities that handle diaspora; "many more states have been experimenting with programmatic

DOI: 10.4018/978-1-5225-7757-7.ch005

Copyright © 2019, IGI Global. Copying or distributing in print or electronic forms without written permission of IGI Global is prohibited.

initiatives to reach out to these populations" (Delano & Gamlen, 2014, P. 43). The authors highlight hybridity without referring to it as hybridity, arguing diaspora politics and immigration policies "disrupt the assumed symmetry of the self-governing national population and its territorial jurisdiction, and give rise to unconventional modes of citizenship and sovereignty not envisioned at Westphalia or imagined as consistent with modern geopolitics since" (Delano & Gamlen, 2014, P. 43). The concept of hybridity, which has been discussed previously, threatens the traditional conception of the nation-state apparatus. Although there are still obvious roles that the nation-state plays, such as militarily, rule of law/governance, and economically – hybridity particularly questions the existence and maintenance of national identity in a post-national (or transnational) world. While some theorists argue that hybridity provides an alternative to the static conception of diaspora as a place of origin, location, and rooted identity (Gilroy, 2000; Mercer, 1994), it is still important to consider the existence (or lack thereof) of an autonomous nation-state in examining contemporary diaspora. Cohen (2008, P. 2) notes a main characteristic of "classical, victim diaspora" or the concept of diffusion of a people following a "traumatic event in the homeland, to two or more foreign destinations" – again this understanding of diaspora is commonly associated with the Jewish people, and scholars tend to discuss a trauma such as the Holocaust, as affecting a group collectively, but as the world has witnessed with more recent diasporic events such as the displacement of Syrian refugees or the migrant crisis in Central Africa – not all people within an ethnic or religious diaspora group are impacted identically. Anthias (1998, P. 564) notes that diasporas are not "homogeneous in another sense: they may have formed different collective representations of the group under local conditions. In addition, the extent to which they organize around cultural symbols, develop ethnic cultural organizations and promote their ethnic identity will be diverse", meaning that the experience of all Jewish, Kurdish, Armenian, Palestinian, etc., will vary depending on the host country and the extent to which other cultures are able to influence the diasporic locals.

In considering diaspora, the role of the nation-state is ever-changing and is dependent on various domestic factors such as the composition of the diaspora; the political type of the regime in the homeland; governmental (formal) and societal (informal) views and opinions on immigration; and citizenship laws. Global factors (or those outside of the host nation) also come to bear in the analysis of diaspora external factors include political type of the host and the existence of national and international organizations (such as the United Nations) (Brand, 2006, 2014). Again the concept of diasporization (Abramson, 2017) comes to bear as the concept emphasizes the "attachment to the homeland from afar and highlights the complexities of home(s), belonging(s), and loyalty(ies)" (P. 15).

## A BRIEF NOTE ON THE PALESTINIAN-ISRAELI CONFLICT

It is impossible to discuss enduring diaspora without acknowledging the Palestinian-Israeli conflict, which for the purposes of this work cannot be dissected in full, as it is a content rich topic that fills libraries. Kodmani-Darwish notes that the Palestinian diaspora is one that is gradual flux, stating,

*The myth of an established diaspora has its virtues. It allows the leaders of the emerging national entity to claim the advantage that will be derived from the educated and flourishing Palestinians' contribution to building the young State. More fundamentally, it may be useful to reformulate in positive terms situations that have been so far perceived as negative experiences. (1997, P. xi)*

The contemporary conflict began after Britain withdrew its forces from Palestine in May 1948. The opposing sides did not reach formal armistice agreements until February of 1949 though the United Nations negotiated two ceasefire agreements during the conflict. Under the armistices (struck between Israel, Egypt, Lebanon, Transjordan, and Syria) border lines were agreed upon. Israel gained territory that was previously granted to Palestinian Arabs under the U.N. resolution in 1946; while Egypt and Jordan retained control over Gaza and the West Bank respectively. The establishment of the nation of Israel, an ethnically-based nation in once Palestinian occupied land caused a displacement of much of the Arab population to neighboring countries and internationally. Numerous wars were fought over the territory and boundaries shifted during the 1970s (Yom Kippur War, 1973), and the Palestinians engaged in violent aggression on Israel dating back to the 1920s and 1930s, which came to bear as the Palestinian Liberation Organization founded in 1964 came to advocate increased violence on the part of the Palestinians, coming to a peak during with the first intifada (1987). This uprising involved hundreds of thousands of Palestinians living in the West Bank and Gaza (CFR, 2018). The Oslo Accords were signed in 1993, bringing an end to the intifada and established an infrastructure to allow the Palestinians to govern themselves and provided for a more cooperative relationship between the Israeli government and the Palestinian Authority. This tenuous peace did not last as the second intifada started in 2000. More recently, in 2015 after an enduring campaign of violence from both sides in the summer of 2014 that left 73 Israelis and 2,251 Palestinians dead, Palestinian President Mahmoud Abbas announced that Palestine was no longer obligated to the Oslo Accords (CFR, 2018).

There has been an increase in hostilities between the Palestinians and Israelis that have only been exacerbated by the election of Donald Trump and foreign policy position switches such as the moving of the U.S. embassy in Israel to Jerusalem. There is great concern among international relations scholars that there may be a third intifada in the future with the intensified tensions, which does seem increasingly likely as the world witnessed the brutal and public killing of more than 50 Palestinians attempt to broach the border wall (Plett Usher, 2018). The Palestinians are a victim diaspora, and have had to struggle for recognition (often that struggle is violent). Cohen argues that victim diasporic populations must cope with a violent displacement from their homeland that resonates so powerfully throughout the group (through generations), that "restoring the homeland or even returning there becomes an important focus for social mobilization, and the mold in which their popular cultures and political attitudes are formed" (2008, P. 4). The conflict between Palestine and Israel has flared up at various times throughout the 20th and into the 21st century, largely due to a generational education centering on Othering from both sides of the conflict. Young Palestinians are taught that Israelis have stolen their homeland and are encroaching on their heritage; while young Israelis are taught just the opposite – that Palestinians are squatting (unlawfully) on their territorial and ancestral homeland and are violently endangering the Israeli right to self-determination and an autonomous state. Frisch grimly summarizes the potential *withering* Palestinian diaspora,

*...Statehood and the building of a state, which could effectively mobilize its diaspora, seem highly unlikely to be achieved in the near future. Instead, as Palestinians ponder their stateless condition, there is a perpetual state of near or actual civil war between the nationalist and Islamist camps in the territory being contested by Israel and the Palestinians, and the destruction of the Palestinian community in Lebanon, which more than any other serves as the symbol of uprooted Palestinian life, continues unabated. (2012, P. 241)*

Safran emphasized the importance of homeland in defining diaspora, he noted, "Members of a diaspora retained a collective memory of *their original homeland*; they idealized their *ancestral home*, were committed to the restoration of *the original homeland* and continued in various ways to *relate to that homeland* (Safran, 1991/2005, emphasis added by author). It is important to bring attention again to how the concept of *home* has evolved throughout diaspora studies (as argued by Cohen, 2008), Brah questions "Where is home?" and goes on to state,

*On the one hand, 'home' is a mythic place of desire in the diasporic imagination. In this sense it is a place of no return, even if it is possible to visit the geographical territory that is seen as the place of 'origin'. On the other hand, home is also the lived experience of a locality. Its sounds and smells, its heat and dust, balmy summer evenings, or the excitement of the first snowfall, shivering winter evenings, somber grey skies in the middle of the day...all this, as mediated by the historically specific everyday of social relations. (1996, P. 183)*

Safran (2005) went further to provide what he considered concrete characteristics of diaspora, though he noted that no contemporary diaspora would meet all of the criteria listed (descriptions of each have been condensed, for a complete characterization, see Safran, 2005, P. 2);

1. Displacement from an original 'centre' to two or more foreign regions;
2. Sustained collective memories, visions, or myths about the original homeland;
3. Diasporic population "believe they are not – and perhaps can never – be fully accepted in their host societies and so remain partly separate";
4. Idealization of the ancestral home and hope to return to home once "conditions are favorable";
5. Adherence to the belief that all members of the diaspora "should be committed to the maintenance or restoration of the original homeland and to its safety..."; and
6. Members of diaspora "continue in various ways to relate to that homeland and their ethnocommunal consciousness and solidarity".

Cohen adapts Safran's essential characteristics of diaspora to include not just the maintenance or restoration of a homeland, but the very creation of a homeland (or a state). He argues that his conceptualization (which is adopted in this work) "covers the cases of *imagined homeland* that only resembles the original history and geography of the diaspora's natality in the remotest way" (this adapted criteria would bring to mind the Kurds, Rohingya Muslims, and Palestinians at the very least) (2008, P. 6). The concept of hybridity can be used by political/social scientists to understand diasporic consciousness, yet critics of hybridity argue that leveling the differences between origin and host country (and societies) leads to a standardization of global politics, thus diaspora politics which need to be dissected in a case-by-case (community-by-community) manner. This argument is similar to Stacey (2018) in which the author highlights the importance of analyzing social movements individually using a historical institutionalism methodology.

Brubaker (2005, P.) throughout the consolidation phase of diaspora studies (which came after Safran's characterization) maintained three core elements that are universally understood of diaspora: 1) "dispersion", whether violently or "voluntarily" typically across state borders; 2) "homeland orientation" to either a real or imagined homeland; and 3) "boundary maintenance", or "the processes whereby group solidarity is mobilized and retained, even accepting that there are counter processes of boundary erosion". This final argument leads to Cohen's more crucial addition to Safran as well as adherence to Brubaker's third element,

*Often mobilize a collective identity, not only a place of settlement or only respect of an imagined, putative or real homeland, but also in solidarity with co-ethnic members in other countries. Bonds of language, religion, culture and a sense of a common fate impregnate such a transnational relationship and give to it an affective, intimate quality that formal citizenship or long settlement frequently lack. (Cohen, 2008, P. 7)*

Diaspora theorist Martin Sökefeld (2006, P. 265) affirms the idea of collective diaspora identity and mobilization, stating, "A diasporic consciousness has, moreover, to be mobilized (that is socially constructed). A significant number of social actors need to accept their collective self-definition as a transnational community, organize to spread this perception and persuade others to participate in actions designed to cement their diasporic character and status". The diasporic consciousness can lead to thinking beyond the boundaries of the nation, Appadurai argues, "The role of intellectual practices is to identify the current crises of the nation and in identifying it to provide part of the apparatus of recognition for post-national social forms" (1996, P. 158). This type of "post-national" diasporic consciousness is arguably necessary in order to mobilize the same community to sociopolitical action (e.g., social movements). Sökefeld, (who will be discussed further in the following chapter) dives into social movement theory to consider the development of diasporic collective identity and communities. He argues that diasporas need opportunity structures in the same manner as a social movement needs an advantageous political, social, or cultural moment to foment dissent, he takes consideration of communication structures in the argument of opportunity structures; diasporic communities need pre-existing social opportunities such as community organizations in order to mobilize participants (again, numerous social movement scholars maintain the necessity of social movement organizations – whether formal or informal); and framing of a message of a homeland, heritage, and a shared history, which helps to invoke solidarity among the community. Cohen (2008, P. 16) reiterates, "A strong or renewed tie to the past or a block to assimilation in the present and future must exist to permit a diasporic consciousness to emerge, while the active fraction of the incipient diasporic must have time to mobilize the group concerned."

Sökefeld's research on diaspora (discussed in Chapter Two) has allowed for more comprehensive analysis of how diasporas are formed, by what types of events, and how do diasporic communities unite and express themselves in places that typically maintain their exclusion from the mainstream population. Further, Chariandy (2007) advocates for a progression of diasporists and diasporic populations to develop tactics similar to social movement organizations to challenge their status. Chariandy argues in hopes,

*...that diaspora studies will help foreground the cultural practices of both forcefully exiled and voluntarily migrant peoples; that diaspora studies will help challenge certain calcified assumptions about ethnic, racial, and above all, national belonging; and that diaspora studies will help forge new links between emergent critical methodologies and contemporary social justice movements. (2007)*

These affective bonds breach gender diaspora politics as discussed in Chapter Four. According to Abramson (2017, P. 16), "Affect – often unconscious and pre-reflexive – has a crucial role in providing a deeper engagement with space, cultivating a sense of belonging to it, and facilitating the imagination of collective memories." Elassi (2015, P. 1) reiterates, "Political belonging creates collective goals to sustain or transform political order", which the world witnessed in relation to the Irish referendum on abortion in 2018. The shared bonds of nationality, politics, and gender were on display in May 2018 when thousands of Irish women (not living in the country) returned to make their voices heard on a referendum on abortion. Silverman (2018) reported that women of Irish descent/nationality returned from places as far away as Australia and the United States to cast their vote. Aided by a hashtag (#HomeToVote), Irish women encouraged one another to repeal the country's eighth amendment to the constitution, which effectively bans abortion. The diaspora of women coming home to vote likely did have an impact on the vote, which came out 66 percent in favoring of repealing the amendment, with an overall voter turnout rate of 64 percent (de Freytas-Tamura, 2018). The Irish diasporic vote emphasizes the development of multiple identities in the host country and in the homeland. The Irish women living abroad felt a kinship to their country women and wanted to exercise their right to vote in a crucial referendum for the future of women's rights in the homeland (that they may or may not return to one day). Arguably the international media and social media platforms played a major role in cultivating a shared Irish female identity on this issue on both sides of the issue (for and against repeal of the amendment), as the transnational diaspora of Irish women became mobilized to participate in this political issue in the homeland.

## TO BE OR NOT TO BE: THE KURDISH STRUGGLE TO DEFINE HOME

But what happens when an individual is part of a diasporic community, identity, and/or consciousness that lacks a recognized state or homeland? How can a collective identity be cultivated from shared experiences without the attachment to a place of origin? This section highlights the contemporary (yet antiquated) struggle of the Kurdish peoples in the Middle East and in diasporic communities around the world. Alinia et al. (2014, P. 53) note that the contemporary Kurdish diasporic communities and "spaces are established as an outcome of the intensified Kurdish migration and relationship with the countries of origin and among Kurds settled in different countries around the globe", yet the Kurds have not achieved self-determination that has been a long-standing goal for the group.

The Kurds origin story is difficult to trace historically, but the first mention of the Kurdish people is during the 7$^{th}$ century, when the group largely converted to Islam and began to mobilize for various causes (and wars) throughout the development of the Middle East, including in the Crusades (Worthington, 2015). The Kurds, throughout history, have been known as a nomadic people as their economy has been dependent upon goats and herding, and arguably this lack of established land became a detriment as the world order shifted and the nation-state became the most important political unit. As borders and sovereign nations popped up around the Kurds, they were relegated to the margins of many societies, which initiated a wave of Kurdish nationalism that began in the late 19$^{th}$ and early 20$^{th}$ centuries.

Between 25 and 35 million Kurds living in a region composed of southeastern Turkey, northeastern Syria, northern Iraq, northwestern Iran, and southwestern parts of Armenia, while roughly 2 million Kurds live outside the Kurdistan region in the diaspora. Although the Kurds are the fourth-largest ethnic group in the Middle East, they have yet to attain an autonomous, sovereign state of their own. Elassi articulates a salient reason why the Kurds remain stateless,

*The sovereign powers in Iran, Iraq, Syria and Turkey for instance do not allow the Kurds to claim a position of statelessness because from the moment the Kurds make a claim to statelessness, they are asserting themselves as political and a challenge to the sovereign state identities in a refusal to be subsumed under their universality. (2015, P. 18)*

The Kurds are a distinctive ethnic group with their own language, race, and cultural traditions, while there is no official religion attached to the group - a majority of Kurds practice Sunni Islam (*BBC*, 2017). The group has been a dominant military presence in the Middle East in the fight against the Islamic State, as IS targeted Kurdish territories in northern Syria early in their campaign to gain land in 2014. The Kurdish military became heavily involved in the fight against the Islamic State in September 2014, when IS fighters took control of Kobane and set in motion a refugee crisis as thousands of Syrian Kurds fled the city to neighboring Turkey (inflaming the hostilities between Turkey and the Kurdish minority). The deeply rooted animosity between Turkey and the Kurds led the Turkish military to not become formally involved in the fight against the Islamic State in Kobane, and instead watched from their border as Syrian Kurds quelled the terrorist organization in 2015. It is important to note that Kurds make up 7 to 10 percent of the Syrian population, and have been (much like in Turkey and elsewhere) relegated to the margins of political and civil society. This military involvement on the part of the Kurds has placed pressure on international allies such as the United States to support statehood for the Kurdish people, and yet there has been no indication that will occur.

The statelessness of the Kurds is a historical struggle (as with most diasporic struggles, it is not modern problem), which began with the fall of the empires in Eurasia, namely the Ottoman Empire. After the fall of the empire and the completion of World War I, the Western allies made arrangements for the establishment of a Kurdish state (Kurdistan) in the Treaty of Sevres (1920), however, that was nullified by the creation of Turkey in the Treaty of Lausanne, and left the Kurds an ethnic minority group in host countries without a homeland. As stated there is significant and long-standing antagonism between Turkey and the Kurdish people who make up 15-20 percent of Turkey's population (*BBC*, 2017). The Kurds throughout history have attempted to create a state, and each time have been out-thwarted. During and after the revolts of the 1920s and 1930s, many Kurds were displaced and resettled by the regime, the government restricted use of the Kurdish language, clothing, customs, and culture in attempt to forcibly assimilate the minority group into greater Turkish society. The government went so far as to deny the existence of the Kurdish ethnic group, instead designating them Mountain Turks (*BBC*, 2017). The Kurdistan Workers' Party or PKK was established in 1978 by Abdullah Ocalan and has been implicated in acts of terrorism and aggression toward the Turkish government over the last four decades of its existence. The BBC (2017) notes that more than 40,000 people have died or been displaced due to the fighting between the Turkish regime and PKK since 1984. There was relative peace during the 1990s as PKK leveled their demands for an independent state (at the cost of Turkish territory), and instead became more a social justice movement for increased civil and human rights within the Turkish state. As Elassi notes,

*Statelessness is thus not only a question of non-existence or obstruction from existing, but it is also about vulnerability and exposure to political and physical violence by the sovereign state. Moreover, the sovereign state denies the stateless the right to claim a political identity that differs from the sovereign identity and defines the stateless people as 'its own people' in order to legitimate political authority and violence in the name of state order. (2015, P. 25)*

In 2013 a ceasefire between the entities was called after decades of tit-for-tat political aggressions. However, that tenuous peace did not last after the PKK accused the Turkish government of detonating a suicide bomb in the town of Suruc (which is predominately Kurdish) and killing 33. Although the bombing was formally blamed on the Islamic State, PKK publicly attacked

Turkish soldiers of being complicit in the act. This allegation led the Turkish government to launch a "synchronized war on terror" against both the Islamic State and PKK (*BBC*, 2017).

The Kurds living in Iraq have fared a bit better than the neighboring countries such as Turkey and Syria yet have still faced incredible hardships in the struggle for recognition and statehood. The Kurds compose 15 to 20 percent of Iraq's population (similar to Turkey), and although the Kurdistan Democratic Party was formed in 1946 in Iraq, it took until the 1970s for Iraqi Kurds to begin an armed fight for self-determination. During the late 1970s, the Iraqi government began resettling the Kurds out of oil rich towns that they established such as Kirkuk and allowing Arab natives to claim the land (thus the resources). The resettlement policy was increased during the Iraq-Iran War in the 1980s when the Kurdistan Democratic Party (thus a majority of the Iraqi Kurds) supported Iran (*BBC*, 2017). In retaliation for supporting Iran, Saddam Hussein initiated a coordinated campaign of chemical weapons attacks on the Kurdish people in 1988. After the Gulf War ended in 1991, the world witnessed as the Iraqi Kurds attempted to gain sovereignty and were violently suppressed by the government, which prompted the United States and allying countries to impose a no-fly zone, allowing the Patriotic Union of Kurdistan (PUK) and Democratic Kurdistan Party (KDP) to self-govern without the interference of the Iraqi regime in Baghdad.

Yet there was tension among the Iraqi Kurds themselves, which led to a four-year war between the PUK and KDP that began in 1994 that subsided when the War on Terror was launched in Iraq. The groups cooperated in getting Hussein out of power and were able to govern the Kurdistan Regional Government (KRG) in coalition. The president of the Kurdistan Regional Government in Iraq announced in early 2017 that a referendum on independence took place on September 25, 2017. Although the referendum simply asked inhabitants of the Kurdistan region if they want an independent state and would not put into place a mechanism for declaring independence, it would signify to Baghdad that the tentative regional structure of governance is at risk, and the Kurds are interested in "pursu[ing] independence more aggressively in a post-Islamic State Iraq" (Kaplan & Mardini, 2017). In the September 25 referendum, 93 percent of the Kurdish electorate voted for independence, with a turnout of over 72 percent (Dalay, 2017), meaning "more than 90 percent of the 3.3 million Kurds who voted supported succession" (*BBC*, 2017). Yet the legitimacy and validity of the vote was dismissed by the Iraqi government, as the sovereignty of the Baghdad government would be affected by the creation of an autonomous Kurdistan. As Dalay notes, the referendum has "put Kurdish aspirations and grievances – both of which risked being overlooked once the fight against ISIS was over and the United States downsized its commitment to Iraq – firmly onto the international agenda" (2017). The vote also raised awareness of how far Baghdad will go to keep its border structure intact, as in October 2017, the Iraqi pro-government forces took over disputed territory that was claimed by the Kurds (including the oil-rich town of Kirkuk), which represents a devastating blow to the self-sufficiency of the Kurds in Iraq and their ability to demand an autonomous state.

The self-determination question for the Kurds is very much in the air as the President of the Iraqi Kurdish Region Masoud Barzani resigned his post on October 29, 2017, after the referendum in September, leaving a void in leadership in the KRG. As well as the uncertain support of international allies like the United States that are willing to support the Kurds when there is a mutual goal (e.g., riding Syria of the Islamic State) yet the West has been reluctant to support the sovereignty of the Kurdish people. In the 2018 elections in Turkey, the Kurds made gains in the legislative branch; the pro-Kurdish, Peoples' Democratic Party, or HDP won almost 12 percent of the 600 seats that comprise the parliament. By Turkish law, political parties must receive above 10 percent of the vote to enter parliament, and if a party falls short of the 10 percent threshold, their votes are redistributed amongst the remaining competitors. The HDP campaigned on a message of greater autonomy for the Kurdish peoples living within Turkey, but are careful to toe the line regarding militant Kurdish nationalism and calls for an independent state. Kurds in Iraq (as noted) are attempting to move toward self-determination but have been sidelined by the Baghdad government, and Kurds in Iran are also mobilizing for autonomy. Members of the Democratic Party of Iranian Kurdistan descended from the mountains in June 2018 and put out a call online for Iranian Kurds to confront the regime in Tehran (Frantzman, 2018). This declaration led the Iranian Revolutionary Guard to launch pre-emptive attacks and deploy military equipment in Kurdish regions of the country, in order to quell any sort of rebellion that may be building. The Iranian Kurds seem to be a bit more political (at least savvy), in recent weeks PDKI's leader Hijri noted that while the group has laid out their case to the Trump administration, the U.S. does not have definitive plans to support the opposition in Iran at this moment (Frantzman, 2018). Although U.S. Secretary of State Mike Pompeo condemned the Revolutionary Guard's attack on the PDKI and the Iranian Kurdish regions on June 27, 2018, the administration has yet to signal increased support to the Kurds and further alienate the government in

Tehran. In Iraq, Iran, and Turkey where the Kurdish people comprise 5-25 percent of the population, the ethnic minority group has been relegated to the sidelines of mainstream political and civil society, living in a diaspora within what they consider to be regions of the Kurdish homeland.

## VIRTUAL DIASPORA: KURDS IN CYBERSPACE

The contemporary Kurdish diaspora has (as other diasporas have) become interconnected in the digital age. Kurdish peoples across the world are able to communicating and establish the ever-important diasporic consciousness that provides for a shared sense of identity, heritage, culture, and society – even if the diasporic members are not in proximity of the homeland (imagined or real). As has been stated by numerous theorists over the last two decades (at least), the efficiency, cost effectiveness, and mobility of digital technologies (accompanied by the internet) have enabled transnational communication and makes the internet and its various mediums, including social media platforms a quintessential tool for non-state actors (interest groups, social movement organizations, civil society associations, and regular people) to become involved in diaspora politics. Kissau and Hunger (2008, P. 15) state, "The internet has aided Diaspora communities to survive, when contact had been lost, numbers of members were too low and individuals too dispersed. In these cases the internet has not only intensified diasporic communication or activities, but has been essential for survival."

Cohen (1997, P. 26) argues for a new definition of diaspora that fits within a new media framework, stating, "Moreover, transnational bonds no longer have to be cemented by migration or by exclusive territorial claims. In the age of cyberspace, a diaspora can, to some degree, be held together or re-created through the mind, through cultural artifacts and through a shared imagination." Mahmod reiterates the importance of the "new media to discuss (strong) transnational links to origin countries and the internet's exploitation of time and space to reinforce national identities across distances and unite scattered populations" (2011, P. 73). Time and space are eliminated in this [networked diaspora] scenario to "reconstitute parts of the community and to exchange cultural knowledge held in the diaspora. Chat sites allow for subscribers, many of whom tend to be of particular ethnic, cultural or religious backgrounds, to communicate from any place where they have access to the internet" (Karim, 2002, P. 276).

Spatiality becomes important to the contemporary definition of diaspora in the digital age, as the internet has blurred the traditional conceptions of space as a fixed location, place of origin, or home, and takes on social, economic, and political connotations (Georgiou, 2010). Particularly Mahmod is interested in the Kurdish identity and diaspora in online communities, and how disparate populations are able to provide for a shared consciousness across borders. Ong (2003) examines the Chinese cyber diaspora and warns of the dangers of a digital discourse as "Internet-based articulation of a disembedded global racial citizenship can create invidious essential differences between ethnic others and natives, deepening rather than reducing already existing political and social divisions within particular nations" (P. 83). However, in contrast, Georgiou (2010) maintains that in this transnational diasporic environment "the domestic, the local, the public, the urban, the national, and the transnational form an interconnected spatial matrix, where possibilities for belonging, for choosing not to belong and for combining belonging in multiple communities emerge" (P. 23). Kok and Rogers (2016) describe the interconnected diaspora communities and digital tools that are used to network as "transglocalization", where the local, national, and transnational community communicates via digital technologies (or online), exist together yet act separately most often.

According to Kissau and Hunger (2008, P. 12), "Transnational communities maintain lasting relationships across borders, agents thereby being not states or nations, but individual actors or associations", which is the hallmark of the online diaspora that exists in the contemporary international community. As Adamson (2001) asserts, "In reality, the increased *diasporization* of ethnic groups around the world is a structural development related to the new opportunities for communication and transportation presented by available technologies" (P. 158). Just as political and social science has had to accommodate the digital technologies and other considerations of the digital age in analyzing topics such as social movements, mobilization, revolution, public policy creation, public opinion, political psychology, etc., so too must comparative scholars (diasporists) accept the role of digital technologies and social media platforms in communicating diaspora and providing for a collective identity among a dispersed ethnic group.

When examining the role of digital technologies and the internet in diaspora studies, Kissau and Hunger (2008, P. 2-3) identify six aspects in which the internet is an asset to members of diasporic communities, including: allowing researchers to view the diasporic community from afar as well as other members of the diasporic community to participate in activities that are specific to the community, such as spreading political awareness, campaigning for candidates, fundraising, etc.; the internet plays a major role in the construction of a shared identity, "internet platforms play a key role in this process as they further the retention or reawakening of identities and imagined homelands" (P. 3); and the internet facilitates the bridging of cultures, politics, and loyalties between home and host countries. Another aspect that Kissau and Hunger note that is underrepresented in much of the literature on diaspora is that diasporic communities are using online forums and websites to document their heritage and attempt to ensure the ethnic group's survival (2008). While it is not enough to simply analyze diasporic communities and politics through digital technologies, a comparative examination is still necessary, however, the internet and social media platforms that provide increased communication among and between diasporic communities should be considered in future diaspora studies. Appandurai (1996, P. 147) refers to the "diasporic public sphere" as a way to denote the existence of varying diasporic civil societies and communities, which is evident in Mahmod's research on the Kurdish digital diaspora.

Mahmod examines threads from online forum *Viva Kurdistan* to paint a picture of the use of social media platforms and digital technologies to reinforce an identity (with or without a homeland). Mahmod asserts that the Kurdish diaspora "an increasing number of individuals who live within multiple cultures, speak multiple languages, and live through transnational practices – are confronting the boundaries by which nations and majority groups define themselves" (2011, P. 5). The internet and digital technologies aid in the linking of the Kurdish (and other) diasporic groups both residing within and outside the homeland, establishing a transnational diasporic community that is connected (communicatively) by the internet but is also attached to a collective identity. Yet as Appadurai (2006) argues negotiating the diasporic identity online can be complicated, "collective imaginings and imagined collectivities, in the era of cyber technologies, are no longer two sides of the same coin. Rather, they frequently test and contest one another" (P. 24).

Viva Kurdistan is one of many online forums, websites, or social media presences of the Kurdish diaspora. This author follows at least one other Kurdish rights group on Twitter, the Kurdistan Solidarity Campaign, which describes itself as a "labour movement and civil society campaign supporting the rights of the Kurdish people to freedom, justice, and equality" (@ KurdsCampaign, 2018). The official Kurdistan Regional Government also has a social media presence on Twitter (although unverified), the account

@Kurdistan has more than 400,000 followers and updates them on official government actions, policies, and press releases pertaining to the Kurds. Viva Kurdistan is a "site of resistance", according to Mahmod, which "can open up liminal spaces from which participants can challenge, criticize and resist regimes, and engage in external or internal power struggles" (2011, P. 76). External issues involve the relationships between Kurds and political regimes under which they live or how the Kurds have built unity and a shared sense of identity. While internal issues to the online forum include the Othering of fellow Kurds, proclaiming someone "not Kurdish enough" because they are not fluent in the language or adopt too many of the host countries customs, norms, and traditions (Mahmod, 2011, P. 77).

Mahmod also investigates cultural norms via the Viva Kurdistan platform and reports in regard to gender roles. Many Kurdish women residing in Western countries are still influenced first and foremost by their relationships with their immediate family, and the traditions that are exhibited to them throughout life. Mahmod notes, "...these online discussions engage predominately those young Kurds who are presumably 'stronger' carriers of a consciousness of the different cultures and norms", as was the sentiment of the Middle Eastern women interviewed in the previous chapter. It is the youth that tend to provide a bridge between host and home countries and the cultures of both. Mahmod concludes,

*In these threads, young women converse about themselves as objects of Kurdish historical and cultural traditions. They reflect on their status as subjects of Western societies that challenge existing categorizations of Kurdish women vis-à-vis the Western vision of femininity and autonomy and vis-à-vis Kurdish men and their individuality. (2011, P. 79)*

As stated, the internet has been a discourse-changing medium for solidifying collective identities and the Kurds are taking advantage of the discursive and communicative opportunities for mobilizing diasporic consciousness, identity, and communities to sociopolitical action. Kissau and Hunger (2008) highlight through their research on Kurdish websites that these digital mediums are used to emphasize the shared cultural heritage and cultivate a shared (collective) Kurdish identity or consciousness, which distinguishes the Kurdish identity from the host country identity (and other ethnic minorities within the host society). Mahmod notes that this contemporary diasporic consciousness would not be possible nor as strong without the availability of digital technologies and social media platforms, "...this sense of the 'imagined community', which

Anderson (2006, P. 6) speaks of in the context of broadcast media, can be envisioned not so much because people will not meet or know each other as Anderson explains, but precisely because people now actually can meet online and be exposed to diversity" (2011, P. 81). The internet has opened up diasporic populations to understanding the differences and similarities between them and how this discovery of differing characters may "change participants' perceptions of the nation, the self, and the personal relationship to Kurdish diasporas" (Mahmod, 2011, P. 81). Kissau and Hunger (2008) conclude a similar study of Kurdish online diasporic communities by noting, "While they communicate with other Kurdish migrants dispersed worldwide, the whole structure of their online interaction and their residence abroad is not stable, as their return to Kurdish areas is a predominant goal" (P. 12).

The internet provides for a diversification of migrant opportunities, not just for leaders or influencers within the diaspora, but for everyday members of the diaspora to interact and communicate with the transnational diasporic community. Transnational diasporic communities that are facilitated online provide a mediated and interconnected space for members to connect with other diasporic members in distant places, providing for greater awareness of the local, national, global and transnational networks available. This interconnected provides for "a world of critical proximity", where members of diasporic communities become aware that "they are not just reflections of their country of origin, they do not belong to a single group, they are not just located in a territory", highlighting the hybridity associated with contemporary diaspora (Georgiou, 2010, P. 30). Transnational diaspora and the required reconfiguration of the concepts of space and collectivity show that "identity is not only about what is inside a group and it is not only about continuity, but it is also about the reinvention of the limits of representation" (Georgiou, 2010, P. 31). Kissau and Hunger note, "Since communication online is non – or – almost non-hierarchical, it lets Diaspora centers become less vivid and their action no longer necessarily focused on a (imagined) homeland" (2008, P. 16). Georgiou (2002, P. 12) reiterates the decentralization of diaspora that the internet provides, "Diasporas cannot only exist as satellites around a center anymore; the power of knowledge and control of information, the responsibility and the active participation in community activities that do not go through the center and which develop beyond control of the center, reflect a new diasporic condition", which is characterized by transnationalism.

The following chapter connects the theories and cases of diaspora discussed throughout this work (territorial/traditional and psychological/sentimental), highlighting the essential aspects of contemporary diaspora. The chapter also provides suggestions for future research in diaspora studies, which is an important field of study in the post-War on Terror international community that is marked by varying conflicts that have exacerbated a global refugee crisis. Diasporic communities and the construction of a collective identity are coloring the current politics of both home and host countries (emigration/immigration policies). Thus it behooves political and social scientists to analyze the development of diaspora consciousness or identity, and how that identity can be harnessed into sociopolitical mobilization.

## REFERENCES

Abramson, Y. (2017). Making a homeland, constructing a diaspora: The case of Taglit-Birthright Israel. *Political Geography*, *58*, 14–23. doi:10.1016/j.polgeo.2017.01.002

Adamson, F. (2001). Mobilizing for the Transformation of Home: Politicized Identities and Transnational Practices. In N. Al-Ali & K. Koser (Eds.), *New Approaches to Migration?: Transnational Communities and the Transformation of Home*. London: Routledge.

Alinia, M., Wahlbeck, Ö., Eliassi, B., & Khayati, K. (2014). The Kurdish diaspora: Transnational ties, home, and politics of belonging. *Nordic Journal of Migration Research*, *4*(2), 53–56. doi:10.2478/njmr-2014-0007

Anderson, B. (2006). *Imagined Communities: Reflections on the Origin and Spread of Nationalism*. London: Verso Books.

Appadurai, A. (1995). The Production of Locality. In R. Fardon (Ed.), Counterworks: Managing the Diversity of Knowledge (pp. 204-225). London: Routledge. doi:10.4324/9780203450994_chapter_10

Appadurai, A. (1996). *Modernity at Large: Cultural Dimensions of Globalization*. Minneapolis, MN: University of Minnesota Press.

Appadurai, A. (2006). The Right to Research. *Globalisation, Societies and Education*, *4*(2), 167–177. doi:10.1080/14767720600750696

BBC News. (2017). *Who are the Kurds?* Accessed from: https://www.bbc.com/news/world-middle-east-29702440

Brah, A. (1996). *Cartographies of Diaspora: Contesting Identities*. London: Routledge.

Brand, L. A. (2006). *Citizens abroad: Emigration and the state in the Middle East and North Africa*. Cambridge, UK: Cambridge University Press. doi:10.1017/CBO9780511491498

Brand, L. A. (2014). Arab uprisings and the changing frontiers of transnational citizenship: Voting from abroad in political transitions. *Political Geography*, *41*, 54–63. doi:10.1016/j.polgeo.2013.11.009

Brubaker, R. (2005). The 'diaspora' diaspora. *Ethnic and Racial Studies*, *28*(1), 1–19. doi:10.1080/0141987042000289997

Chariandy, D. (2007). *Soucouyant*. Vancouver: Arsenal Pulp Press.

Cohen, R. (1997/2008). *Global Diasporas: An Introduction*. London: University College London Press. doi:10.4324/9780203228920

Council on Foreign Relations. (2018). *Israeli-Palestinian Conflict*. Accessed from: https://www.cfr.org/israeli-palestinian-conflict

Dalay, G. (2017). After the Kurdish Independence Referendum. *Foreign Affairs*. Accessed from https://www.foreignaffairs.com/articles/middle-east/2017-10-02/after-kurdish-independence-referendum

De Freytas-Tamura, K. (2018). Ireland Votes to End Abortion Ban in Rebuke to Catholic Conservatism. *New York Times*. Accessed from: https://www.nytimes.com/2018/05/26/world/europe/ireland-abortion-yes.html

Délano, A., & Gamlen, A. (2014). Comparing and Theorizing State–diaspora Relations. *Political Geography*, *41*, 43–53. doi:10.1016/j.polgeo.2014.05.005

Elassi, B. (2015). *Narratives of Statelessness and Political Belonging Among Kurdish Diasporas in Sweden and the UK*. International Migration Institute, Working Paper 114, Oxford University.

Frantzman, S. (2018). Iranian Kurds Increase Campaign Against Tehran Regime. *Jerusalem Post*. Accessed from: https://www.jpost.com/Middle-East/Iranian-Kurds-increase-campaign-against-Tehran-regime-561800

Frisch, H. (2012). The Demise of the PLO: Neither Diaspora nor Statehood. *Political Science Quarterly*, *127*(2), 241–261. doi:10.1002/j.1538-165X.2012.tb00726.x

Gamlen, A., Cummings, M., Vaaler, P., & Rossouw, L. (2013). *Explaining the rise of diaspora institutions*. Working Paper 78. International Migration Institute, University of Oxford.

Georgiou, M. (2002). *Diasporic Communities On-Line. A Bottom Up Experience of Transnationalism*. Journal Hommes et Migrations.

Georgiou, M. (2010). Identity, Space and the Media: Thinking through Diaspora. *Revue Européenne des Migrations Internationales*, *26*(1), 17–35. doi:10.4000/remi.5028

Gilroy, P. (2000). *Between Camps*. London: Allen Lane.

Kaplan, M., & Mardini, R. (2017). The Kurdish Region of Iraq is Going to Vote on Independence. Here's What You Need to Know. *Washington Post*. Accessed from: https://www.washingtonpost.com/news/monkey-cage/wp/2017/06/21/what-you-need-to-know-about-the-kurdish-referendum-on-independence/?utm_term=.1812c51339e6

Karim, K. (Ed.). (2002). *The Media of Diaspora*. London: Routledge.

Kissau, K., & Hunger, U. (2008). *The Internet as a means of studying transnationalism and Diaspora?* Paper presented at Diaspora and Transnationalism Conceptual, Theoretical and Methodological Challenges, European University Institute.

Kodmani-Darwish, B. (1997). *La Diaspora Palestinienne*. Paris: Presses universitaires de France.

Kok, S., & Rogers, R. (2016). Rethinking Migration in the Digital Age: Transglocalization and the Somali Diaspora. *Global Networks*, *17*(1), 23–46. doi:10.1111/glob.12127

Mahmod, J. (2011). Designing Scripts and Performing Kurdishness in Diaspora: The Online-Offline Nexus. *Cultural Policy, Criticism, and Management Research*, *5*, 72–90.

Ong, A. (2003). Cyberpublics and Diaspora Politics among Transnational Chinese. *Interventions*, *5*(1), 82–100. doi:10.1080/1369803200049815

Plett-Usher, B. (2018). Jerusalem Embassy: Why Trump's Move Was Not About Peace. *BBC News*. Accessed from: https://www.bbc.com/news/world-us-canada-44120428

Safran, W. (1991). Diasporas in modern societies: Myths of homeland and return. *Diaspora, 1*(1), 83–99. doi:10.1353/dsp.1991.0004

Safran, W. (2005). The Jewish Diaspora in a comparative and theoretical perspective. *Israel Studies, 10*(1), 36–60. doi:10.2979/ISR.2005.10.1.36

Silverman, R. (n.d.). The Irish Diaspora Flocking Home in the Hope of Swinging the Historic Abortion Referendum. *The Telegraph.* Accessed from: http://www.telegraph.co.uk/women/politics/irish-diaspora-flocking-home-hope-swinging-historic-abortion/

Sökefeld, M. (2006). Mobilizing in transnational space: A social movement approach to the formation of diaspora. *Global Networks*, *6*(3), 265–284. doi:10.1111/j.1471-0374.2006.00144.x

Stacey, E. (2018). *Nationalism, Social Movements, and Activism: Emerging Research and Opportunities*. IGI Global. doi:10.4018/978-1-5225-5433-2

# Chapter 6
# Connecting Diasporic Threads and Suggestions for Future Research


## ABSTRACT

*This chapter summarizes the classical (or old) and psychological/affective (or new) characterization of diaspora and the establishment of diasporic communities in the modern age. The chapter provides greater insight into the role of the nation-state in diasporic relations in the contemporary transnational community. The author provides suggestions for future research on diaspora and diasporic political mobilization and recommends a greater focus on comparative analysis of diasporic communities which would provide for an increased awareness of the differences among diasporas and the struggles those communities face in both homeland and host country.*


## INTRODUCTION

This chapter will emphasize the connective threads between political and psychological conceptions of diaspora as presented in this work and provide theorists with suggestions for future research on global diaspora politics and the ability to mobilize dispersed populations for social change. Definitions of diaspora and what constitutes a diasporic community have evolved over time in response to individual as well as global designations of diaspora, yet there has been an essential constant underlying, which is the notion of a

DOI: 10.4018/978-1-5225-7757-7.ch006

Copyright © 2019, IGI Global. Copying or distributing in print or electronic forms without written permission of IGI Global is prohibited.

homeland (real or imagined) and the necessity of that homeland to cultivate a diasporic collective identity or consciousness that is obligatory for mobilization of a dispersed people. As diaspora studies adapts to the digital age, the characterization and definition of diaspora have expanded (begrudgingly to some theorists) to include psychological aspects of diaspora such as feelings of belonging, gender, and the varied concept of home and what it means in a transnational world. Another important feature of the transnational (digital) diasporic community is the lessened focus on place as a fixed location and an increased emphasis on the imagination and affective nature of diaspora. As Giddens (1990) asserts once space ceases to be a singular focal point for social relations (or on which social relations are established), diasporic members are able to free themselves of the burdens of place and expand the potential for communication and development of a community (thus, a collective identity based around more than just a common place of origin).

Diaspora as a concept suggests a multitude of connections across the diasporic community (those who are residing in the homeland and those living outside in host countries), which implies varied connections and networks developed across nation-state borders. Diasporas are an interesting topic of inquiry as the diasporic nature detaches ethnic identity from a singular place of origin (most often, a nation-state) and introduces the potential for multiple identities that are based around host and home society. Dispersed peoples generally present a risk to the (often nearly) homogeneous nation-state and "call into question the idea that a people [must] have a land in order to be a people" (Boyarin & Boyarin, 1993, P. 718). With the influx of digital technologies and a shifting of the traditional media infrastructure, diasporic communities are better equipped than any point in history to develop viable networks of communication and shared identity. Diaspora presumes the mobility not just of peoples but, of ideas, discourse, and the resettlement of a people (and heritage) in a host country.

The study of diaspora and condition of living within it has become more interconnected due to the new media technologies that allow for the quick dissemination of political ideology, reinforcing of traditions and norms, and eschewing the host country civil society infrastructure. This work has focused on two distinct notions of diaspora; a political or territorial definition that is characterized by the adherence to a homeland (place of origin, whether real or imagined) and a psychological or affective perspective, which emphasizes the importance of sentiments such as belonging as well as engages in a conversation regarding gender diaspora (which is felt not just by women living in diaspora, but can be felt by women living in their homeland due to the distance and standards placed on femaleness over that of being a male in Western societies). In both instances of diaspora, new media has been incorporated into the mobilization tactics of leaders and the new generation of members (within various diasporic communities). Arguably this infusion of available digital technologies coupled with the internet has altered the manner in which diasporic communities are able to cultivate a shared identity and solidify the heritage and attachments (traditions, norms, culture, etc.) of the homeland (real or imagined).

## OLD VS. NEW DIASPORA

As has been noted throughout this work, the conception of diaspora has evolved throughout time and experiences of various peoples from *old* to *new* characterizations of what constitutes a diaspora, and how to mobilize diasporic communities for sociopolitical change. The old diaspora is characterized by essential notions of the migration of a people (often forcibly and involuntarily) and that peoples' concentration on returning to that homeland (real or imagined). Van Amersfoort characterizes classical diaspora,

*The classical diasporas were a phenomenon produced by a pre- modern type of political order. They were part of a feudal political arrangement in which "outsiders" performed economic functions in trade and finance that were forbidden to the "insiders"... [Classical] Diaspora cultures reflect this particularistic world; they do not aim at incorporating others or being incorporated by others. (2004, P. 362)*

Cases of old diaspora include the classical Palestinian-Israeli conflict, the Kurdish question of self-determination, and the plight of the Armenians. Classical (old) characterizations of diaspora centered on the concept of home or place of origin, as well as the notion of a longing to return to that homeland from which the diasporic community was displaced. There is a tendency for old diaspora theories to rely heavily on the construction of an ethnic identity as opposed to a cultural or transnational identity that characterizes the new diaspora. Jacobsen notes that boundaries are now perceived to be more permeable, and simultaneously there has been an erosion of territory as the foremost indicator of community or belonging (2002).

While new diaspora and studies on contemporary diaspora place an increased focus on the construction of a shared identity, affective responses to diaspora, as well as transnational aspects of modern diaspora, which allow (if not mandate) diasporic populations to adopt culture, ideology, language, etc., from multiple nation-states and different diasporic communities (homeland, host country, and/or other countries' diasporas). Lie articulates the demarcation between old and new diaspora,

*It is no longer assumed that immigrants make a sharp break from their homelands. Rather, pre-migration networks, cultures, and capital remain silent. The sojourn itself is neither unidirectional nor final. Movements follow multifarious trajectories and sustain diverse networks. Rather than the singular immigrant, scholars now detail the diversity of immigration circumstances, class backgrounds, gendered transitions, and the sheer multitude of migration experiences. (1995, P. 304)*

In examining new (transnational) diaspora, Ostergaard-Nielson summarizes that diaspora activities in relation to host and home country "must be measured with a more finely meshed tool than is usually the case in the analysis of political change at domestic and international levels" (2002, P. 200), as will be argued in the following section. This author believes that the internet and digital technologies are the communicative opportunity for diasporic communities to identity others within their community from across borders and develop a collectivity, which assists in fomenting mobilization via pre-established network of supporters (or diasporic members). Thus the analysis of the internet, social media platforms, and online forums, their uses and the emerging communication networks can provide awareness of migrant behavior and building connections between host and home countries, as well as the differences and similarities of transnational communities and diaspora (Kissau & Hunger, 2008). As Georgiou notes, "The internet has allowed most of these communities to discover and rediscover this shared imagination and commonality; it has taken even further the potentials for developing diasporic cultures of mediated, transnational and partly free from state control communication" (2002, P. 3).

According to Anthias (1998, P. 577), "Diaspora [studies] has [have] turned the gaze to broader social relations that can encompass politics, economy and culture at the global, rather than national level." Yet this does not negate the role that concepts of home, gender, race, and ethnicity play on the dynamics of diasporic communities and the way in which those communities are mobilized. To this point, Hiller and Franz (2001, P. 733) argue, "It is not only past memories and old ties that produce a sense of belonging and rootedness in a territorial homeland, but also how new ties can be discovered and nurtured because of a common identity that is based on a former place of residence." The contemporary (digital) diaspora presumes that the diasporic connections and networks are developed and maintained via the internet and social media platforms that have become tools of discourse between dispersed populations. No longer is returning home a matter of economics (having the money to travel), nor is it a matter of time, with the integration of diasporic communities in the online realm maintaining homeland connections "...can be an intimate aspect of daily living due to the choices that are available in participating in virtual communities" (Hiller & Franz, 2001, P. 735).

Hiller and Franz (2001) articulate three phases of migrant use of the internet to maintain diasporic networks, 1) pre-migrant; 2) post-migrant; and 3) settled migrant, through the phases and examination of different digital tools, the authors explain how diasporas are solidifying bonds in a transnational world. For example, use of email becomes much more nuanced as the individual moves from the pre-to-settled phases of the migration experience; in the *pre-migration* phase it is used to communication with formal or informal contact with "previously known or unknown persons" as a means to "evaluate migration prospects, mobilize assistance, and establish new ties"; *post-migration,* email is primarily used as a means of maintaining contact with the homeland and establish or maintain communication with other members of the diasporic community; and in the *settled* phase, email is used for "communicating with people from home particularly to share life histories and genealogies", this is crucial to maintaining ties to the community and/or homeland (P. 739).

Where communication and the facilitation of diasporic networks was expensive and difficult pre-digital age, the proliferation of the internet, social media platforms, email and SMS capabilities and increased accessibility has strengthened diasporic communities around the world. Diasporic populations are better equipped to share ideology, culture, values, and reinforce a collective identity across nations and generations. Old and new characterizations of diaspora (political/territorial vs. transnational) benefit from the infusion of digital technologies, as these tools are being used to not only establish new ties and facilitate new diaspora politics, but also to bolster pre-existing (old) connections and maintain a link to home. As Hiller and Franz argue, "Keeping in contact with family and friends from the region of origin helps to perpetuate a sense of belonging...Old ties are primarily expressive and affective, dealing with emotional linkages, reminiscence and often childhood and family history" (2001, P. 743). Thus old ties (and conceptions of diaspora) are still important to the contemporary characterization of diaspora, yet there is a shifted emphasis on home (nation-state, place of origin) as a signifier of identity. According to O Tuathail, the risk of disassociating the nation-state from diaspora brings about challenges

*...to the status of territory, and by extension, our territorially embedded understandings of geography, governance and geopolitics, states, places, and the social sciences, by planetary communication networks and globalizing tendencies...The problematic of deterritorialization is also the problematic of reterritorialization; it is not the presence or absence of state territoriality but its changing status, power and meaning in relationship to postmodern technological constellations, speed machines and global webs of capitalism. (1998, P. 82)*

The erection of diasporic identity in the transnational global environment allows for greater consideration of affective, sentimental, and psychological aspects of both belonging and a sense of home beyond a fixed location (but without negating that place). Hiller and Franz reiterate this idea, noting, "... the online community [is not] independent of a larger community that exists in a physical space...instead [the internet/social media platforms] computer-mediated communication builds an online community from a generalized sense of belonging based on a group identity and a territorial homeland and reinforces it through online interaction" (2001, P. 748). The following section suggests new methods and considerations for political and social scientists researching contemporary diaspora and diasporic community mobilization. Research on diaspora continues to be abundant, yet there is still a need for more thorough comparative analysis on the varying diasporas, their communication discourses and networks established via these discourses, the role of home and host country politics in defining the diasporic consciousness, and how that consciousness leads to mobilization of the diaspora for sociopolitical change.

## SUGGESTIONS FOR FUTURE RESEARCH

Delano and Gamlen note a void in contemporary diaspora studies of comparative work, as well as emphasizing that future research on diaspora needs to broaden to a more complete analysis, particularly featuring mixed methods and interdisciplinary approaches to the subject. Diaspora studies have been quick to declare the state as the central foci of analysis, by focusing on the role of homeland and host countries, traditional diasporists have neglected a more human element as well as the role of non-governmental organizations in diaspora politics (such as social movements). Diaspora political analysis must focus in the future on the actors, sentiment, and forms of contention that are inherent to diaspora. It is important to not only focus on the politics and policies of the host country, but to consider the homeland and how the regime may be encouraging migrant integration and benefitting from diasporic communities. Here there is ample opportunity to identify policies that could be advantageous to both home and host country by providing for a transnational dialogue on immigration and diaspora. As Beck and Sznaider warn,

*Methodological nationalism takes the following premises for granted: it equates societies with nation-state societies and sees states and their governments as the primary focus of social-scientific analysis. It assumes that humanity is naturally divided into a limited number of nations, which organize themselves internally as nation-states and externally set boundaries to distinguish themselves from other nation-states. And it goes further: this outer delimitation as well as the competition between nation-states, represent the most fundamental category of political organization. (2010, P. 382)*

Research in the future should also focus on ethnography and the telling of stories by the diasporic community members themselves. In this approach, research becomes more intimate and biases can be erased by first-hand (primary) accounts of diaspora, particularly in relation to the migrants' experiences with the host society and its citizens. Most Americans, for example, believe themselves to be open-minded and tolerant and would express that if approached for an interview with a political scientist or member of the media. Yet if you inquire about discrimination or harassment with a member of the immigrant (diasporic) population, one would likely be told of a harsh environment that is not as welcoming as the American participant would conceive. Koinova argues that diaspora scholars "have paid little attention to how the radical right affects transnational diaspora mobilization" (2016, P. 505), this is true and increasingly becoming a pressing question in terms of immigration and refugee policies due to a contemporary wave of nationalism (see Stacey, 2018). This nationalism has a profound impact on diasporic communities living within host nations such as the United States, and on how relations between and among diverse groups are represented within a democracy (or other political regime). As Spivak (1993, P. 773) noted, "In the field of rational analysis, a feeling of recognized kinship is more desirable than nationalism." Finally, future research also needs to be more inclusive of contemporary conceptions of diaspora, which include (as this work has focused on) affective or sentimental aspects of diaspora.

It is important to approach diaspora not simply from clinical definitions of location, boundaries, or immigration, and also discuss feelings of belonging, the reasons for migration, and the politics (and policies) of both home and host country that contribute to diaspora. The suggested approaches for future research deemphasize the nation-state as the central object of analysis to consider different non-traditional aspects of diaspora that fit within a comparative research method. This assumes that new research will have increased focus on transnationalism, which tends to assume a different role for the state, national identity adherence, and citizenship regarding diaspora. Karim (2002, P. 277), "The concept of citizenship with respect to a single country is becoming increasingly strained under these circumstances. People who have diasporic connections around the world tend to view themselves as citizens of the world." Thus, the establishment of a diasporic identity or consciousness should be another focal point of future research in regards to the mobilization of diasporic communities in dissent, and/or participation in the larger politics of both home and host countries. Again, the affective nature of diaspora comes into play as constructing collective identities assumes shared memories of heritage, traditions, norms, customs, and often more concrete factors such as politics or religion. In regards to gender, this author will simply reiterate Anthias (1998, P. 572-3), in noting, "more substantive work is needed to research the extent to which diasporic or racialized groups (like all subordinated social groups including those of class), may be subjected to two sets of gender relations: those of the dominant society and those internal to the group." This author attempted to provide such analysis through the interviews with women living within the American-Muslim diaspora, but much more thorough research must be conducted and on a cross-national, comparative scale.

Diaspora studies should take into consideration interdisciplinary and comparative approaches to research, not simply focusing on the state-diaspora relationship but on the dispersed people, and their experiences of diaspora. This includes greater inquiry into the youth diasporic populations and how the young are able to cope with host and homeland country politics and society. This would also provide greater insight as to how the diasporic communities will develop and sustain into the future. To better understand the differences and similarities between diasporic communities, a methodological approach such as historical institutionalism provides a greater awareness to the underlying causes of migration and resettlement politics. Thus research in the future needs to underscore both the importance of and opportunities for diasporic communities to transcend the nation-state infrastructure. While the concept of a homeland (nation-state, real or imagined) is critical to the understanding of diaspora politics, there are many ways in which to dissect the role of the homeland in diasporic mobilization and engagement that have thus far been underscored, such as the emotional or affective relationship to the homeland and diasporic consciousness.

There is a need to re-focus diaspora politics and mobilization in a transnational light in the digital international community, yet it is still important for theorists to consider the role of the state in providing opportunities, policies, and discursive opportunities for diasporic mobilization. As Dickinson notes the notion of homeland (in a symbolic, territorial, and affective way) is still critical to the study of diaspora, "in order to perpetuate a sense of a collective identity sustained by reference to common memories or myths about an ancestral homeland's location, history and achievements" (2014, P. 33). To reiterate, this author argues for an increased focus on transnationalism and digital technologies in diaspora studies that "delimits a certain space as a territory, links that space with society, and harnesses its latent emotional quality" (Abramson, 2017, P. 16), while recognizing the crucial role that the homeland plays in diaspora and diasporic identity/consciousness. Transnationalism as an object of analysis in relation to diaspora emphasizes the potential development of significant relationships and sociopolitical associations across borders and solidifying diasporic networks. These networks will be important for future research in diasporic studies in the digital (and post-digital) age. As Hiller and Franz conclude, "...It is clear that the virtual community provides a variety of forms of social capital, both online and offline, which assists in the migration transition" (2001, P. 749).

The concluding chapter follows and will provide the final word on modern characterizations of diaspora politics and reiterate the importance of both Blumer (1971) and Sökefeld's (2006) theories on mobilization (on social problems and diasporas, respectively). The chapter will also highlight contemporary diaspora concepts such as hybridity and transnationalism, and the role of the digital media in providing for establishing and maintaining diasporic consciousness across borders.

## REFERENCES

Abramson, Y. (2017). Making a homeland, constructing a diaspora: The case of Taglit-Birthright Israel. *Political Geography*, *58*, 14–23. doi:10.1016/j.polgeo.2017.01.002

Anthias, F. (1998). Evaluating Diaspora: Beyond Ethnicity? *Sociology*, *32*(3), 557–580.

Beck, U., & Sznaider, N. (2010). Unpacking cosmopolitanism for the social sciences: a research agenda. *The British Journal of Sociology,* 351-403.

Boyarin, D., & Boyarin, J. (1993). Generation and the Ground of Jewish Identity. *Critical Inquiry*, *19*(4), 693–725. doi:10.1086/448694

Dickinson, J. (2014). Making Space for India in Post-Apartheid South Africa: Narrating Diasporic Subjectivities Through Classical Song and Dance. *Emotion, Space and Society*, *13*, 32–39. doi:10.1016/j.emospa.2014.05.001

Georgiou, M. (2002). *Diasporic Communities On-Line. A Bottom Up Experience of Transnationalism*. Journal Hommes et Migrations.

Giddens, A. (1990). *The Consequences of Modernity*. Stanford, CA: Stanford University Press.

Hiller, H., & Franz, T. (2001). New Ties, Old Ties and Lost Ties: The Use of the Internet in Diaspora. *New Media & Society*, *6*(6), 731–752. doi:10.1177/146144804044327

Karim, K. (Ed.). (2002). *The Media of Diaspora*. London: Routledge.

Koinova, M. (2016). Sustained vs. episodic mobilization among conflict-generated diasporas. *International Political Science Review*, *37*(4), 500–516. doi:10.1177/0192512115591641

Kumar, P. (2018). Rerouting the Narrative: Mapping the Online Identity Politics of the Tamil and Palestinian Diaspora. Social Media Society, 4(1).

Lie, J. (1995). From International Migration to Transnational Diaspora. *Contemporary Sociology*, *24*(4), 303–306. doi:10.2307/2077625

Østergaard-Nielsen, E. (2002). Continuities and changes in sending country perceptions, policies and transnational relations with nationals abroad. In E. Østergaard-Nielsen (Ed.), *International migration and sending Countries: Perceptions, policies and transnational relations*. Hampshire, NY: Palgrave Macmillan.

Spivak, G. (1993). *Outside in the Teaching Machine*. New York: Routledge.

Stacey, E. (2018). *Nationalism, Social Movements, and Activism: Emerging Research and Opportunities*. IGI Global. doi:10.4018/978-1-5225-5433-2

Tuathail, O. G. (1998). Postmodern Politics? The Modern Geopolitical Imagination and Beyond. In Rethinking Geopolitics. London: Routledge.

Van Amersfoort, J. (2004). Gabriel Sheffer and the Diaspora Experience. *Diaspora*, *13*(2), 359–373. doi:10.1353/dsp.2008.0009

# Conclusion

The research presented in this text provides a view into the contemporary diaspora and the politics associated with dispersed populations. The author suggests a new dichotomy for considering and characterizing diaspora in the digital age, namely distinguishing between traditional (or territorial) diaspora and psychological (or affective) diaspora, and the similarities and differences among them. Diaspora politics as a field of study has experienced a reawakening in that while the nation-state (and tone regarding immigration/migration) still plays an important role, that role has been subverted by digital technologies that allow for the development and maintenance of diasporic networks around the world, as well as fomenting of diasporic mobilization for change (often greater recognition by host country or self-determination, as presented in this work). Understanding and providing awareness of global (and perhaps more importantly local) diasporas will be critical in the very near future, as the international community witnesses a surge in refugee migration that shows no signs of slowing. As Cho asserts,

*The turn to diaspora in contemporary criticism is more than just a faddish adoption of a new critical language for the sake of newness. The turn to diaspora signals a demand for finding a way to speak about the complexities of connections between communities, of the unredressed griefs and disarticulated longings from which collectivities emerge. (2007, P. 13)*

Diaspora, as highlighted throughout this work, bring together communities that are not quite based on national identity, nor race, nor religion, nor belonging, but have a connection to each of these concepts, and often a homeland that may or may not exist in the international community. Adamson notes,

*...since attachment to a real or imagined homeland is difficult to measure and subject to change. Not all those who migrate from one place to another maintain a strong connection with the place they left. And yet, many people can feel a strong personal, emotional, and political identification with a real or imagined homeland that they have never lived in or even set foot in—some diaspora activists are several generations removed from their "homeland." (2016, P. 292)*

Diasporic communities through sustained ties and networks have power that can influence political and social decisions in both the home and host country if harnessed at a politically advantageous moment (political opportunity theory). As has been highlighted, mobilization of diasporic communities mirrors much of social movement and political mobilization theories promulgated by political sociologists and comparative theorists for decades (Tilly; Castells; Skocpol; Blumer; Sökefeld). The proliferation and infusion of digital technologies, the internet, and social media platforms has certainly aided the fostering of a collective identity (whether based on ideology, goals, or a shared heritage), which in turn can lead to sustained mobilization of the diasporic community (in both home and host countries). Speaking before the introduction of more sophisticated and seamless communicative platforms (such as Twitter and Facebook), Mandaville articulates the potential of the digital age to impact diasporic communities,

*...diasporic media can and should be understood as much more than simply a means by which information of interest to a given community can be exchanged, or a means for communicating images of that community to the wider society.... We need to understand these media as spaces of communication in which the identity, meaning and boundaries of diasporic community are continually constructed, debated and reimagined. (2001, P. 169)*

According to Cohen (1997, P. 9-10), "In the age of cyberspace, a diaspora can, to some degree, be held together or re-created through the mind, through cultural artefacts and through a shared imagination...This reconstitution of identity threatens the nation-state by a form of semi-detachment or indifference." Sökefeld notes, "Without communication facilities the chance of a dispersed collection of people developing a shared imagination of community is rather small." Thus more digital sociology and political studies using content and network analysis as most recently seen in Kumar (2018) need to be incorporated in future research to provide greater insight into how these diasporic communities are engaging online and how mobilization is accomplished via digital technologies (in the same way that social movement theory had to adapt to the digital era and provide for the changing processes of communicative action).

While some theorists (Cho, 2007; Cohen, 2008) argue against the less concrete characterization of diaspora, noting the irreplaceability of the nation-state as a central focus of analysis, it is worth reiterating that the transnational diaspora is less dependent on a fixed place of origin – as diasporic communities are scattered amongst varied populations, including in the region perceived of as *home*. It is true that this author has argued and maintains that the nation-state remains a crucial aspect of diaspora studies, in looking at the new definitions of diaspora (which has been expanded to include identity-based, race-based, culture-based, and gender-based ideations of diaspora) it is critical for theorists not to overstate the role of nation-state, while making sure not to neglect the policies and politics that contribute to the maintenance of diasporas around the world.

The concluding section synthesizes social movement theories promulgated by Herbert Blumer (life cycle of social problems thesis presented in Chapter Three) and the diasporic mobilization theory of Martin Sökefeld to present an updated theory on the development of diasporic networks and the fomenting of mobilization among displaced populations across the international community. It is the opinion of this author that understanding the movement and facilitation of protest/dissent among diasporic communities will be of the utmost importance as Western countries have increasingly accepted (or tolerated) refugees and migrants from scattered lands, yet as stated there has been an influx of nationalist (and more ideologically conservative) politics (and policies) around the world that is imposing upon the safety and security of diasporic populations (the Othering of Muslims, Hispanic or Latino populations, Africans, peoples without an internationally recognized homeland, women, etc.). Former U.S. Secretary of State Hillary Clinton spoke at the Global Diaspora Forum in 2011, noting,

*... more than 60 million Americans are first- or second-generation members of the diaspora community, and that's a lot of potential. And we need to expand and deepen what's already going on. I know that there is so much that is an ongoing part of the daily lives of the communities that you come from.*

The following (and final) section will provide concluding remarks on the nature of contemporary diasporic communities and how those dispersed groups are able to establish and maintain a collective identity, as well as mobilize these communities for sociopolitical action. The author turns to Sökefeld (2006) and Blumer (1971) a final time to reiterate the importance of not simply viewing diasporas as groups of peoples, but as a process of negotiation and re-negotiation diasporic identity and/or consciousness in relation to both host country and homeland.

## DIASPORIC AND SOCIAL MOVEMENT MOBILIZATION IN THE FUTURE

Diaspora and social movement mobilization have numerous commonalities, but among the most important is the construction of a collective identity (in traditional diaspora, this is conceived of as a home or national identity; in new diaspora and social movements, that identity is more loosely organized around culture, gender, race, ethnicity, etc.). Sökefeld notes that the "concept of framing also takes up the importance of culture, meaning and ideology, which the new social movements approach has emphasized. Melucci points out that movements not only develop within certain contextual frames but that they also 'fashion new meanings for social action'" (2006, P. 270). These frames are critical in the building of a shared identity and the mobilization of social movement and diasporic networks alike. Sökefeld goes onto to note, "Framing processes establish not only the significance of the imagined community but may also refer to specific events that are then defined as incidents that affect the whole community and that thereby trigger the formation of a diaspora community" (2006, P. 204).

Sökefeld's focus on three dominant theories within social movement literatures (political opportunity, framing, and mobilization) provides a bridge between his research on diasporic communities and social movements. Koppmans and Statham (2002) demonstrated that the arrangement of political and institutional resources that are available in host countries in part determines the strategies of diasporic organizations, as well as their claims and goals in mobilization. Diasporic (and social movements) must have opportunities to develop networks and sustain those networks via available technologies, which would fit into Blumer's conception of becoming aware of a social problem and mobilizing a network of dissent. Diasporic communities and social movements find these opportunities via policy actions, electoral maladies, and social reforms, as diasporic members and native citizens (in home and host countries) are stirred to action via an organized network of individuals with a collective identity (and mutual concerns/goals). Sökefeld emphasizes the necessity of framing the diasporic (social movement) identity and messages, noting, "frames include all the ideas from which an imagination of community is composed, the ideas that define migrants as members of a transnational community or relationships as relations of belonging (2006, P. 272). Identity formation is a key pre-cursor to social movement and diasporic mobilization; in order for social and political problems to become mobilizing agents there must be a community to organize around common solutions or reforms. Vertovec (1999) asserts that there can be no diaspora community without a consciousness of diaspora, in other words without an idea of shared identity, of common belonging to a group. Thus there can be no mobilization without the clear existence of a diasporic consciousness that is individual to each diasporic community and their politics (in home and host country).

The bureaucratization phase that Blumer promulgates in his life cycle of social problems thesis may indeed still be relevant in discussing diaspora, which is a departure from what this author has argued in terms of contemporary (networked) social movements. It is arguable that in order for diasporic communities to establish and maintain networks across varied countries - there needs to be some organizational features of the diaspora. These need not be institutionalized or formal entities of the state, rather it is more likely that this organization will come in the form of non-governmental organizations and civil society groups that have a vested interest in distinguishing diaspora politics from domestic politics (of the host country) and mobilizing the wider diasporic network into political action. Organizations such as the Council on American-Islamic Relations, the Council for Arab-West Understanding, National Association for the Advancement of Colored People, The National Institute for Latino Policy, Migration Policy Institute, and particularly local chapters of these (and various other) organizations are drivers of diasporic relations and politics for varied diasporic communities within the United States and beyond and provide diasporic populations with opportunities to mobilize under a shared identity and message. Sökefeld notes,

*People form networks through which the initiative for collective action is spread; and they establish associations that create and sustain discourses of community and that organize mobilizing practices like demonstrations and various community conventions. Such networks and associations can be very diverse; they may be situated at the local level (such as neighborhood community associations) but they also include high-level associations that are themselves of a transnational character. (2006, P. 270)*

There is arguably not a decline phase in relation to diasporic communities and their mobilization as is theorized in social movement literature. As noted in Chapter Three, the decline phase for social movements can take on various forms, including co-option of movement goals and ideology into the mission of the government, or the mainstreaming of that same ideology into the social consciousness, adding pressure to elected officials to make reforms. Because the nature of diaspora is based around a shared identity and the maintenance of a community/network based around that identity (as opposed to specific sociopolitical reforms as in social movements) there is not decline of diasporic consciousness, but perhaps their mobilization for various causes at necessary times. The concept of community is not necessarily fixed, and as Sökefeld (2006) argues must be recreated time and again in order for that community to be politically and socially effective. To reiterate, social movements tend to rely on a more fluid collective identity based around shared beliefs and ideology (political, social, etc.) such as liberalism or socialism, where diasporic mobilization is dependent upon a collective identity based around more fixed identifying concepts (e.g., race, ethnicity, religion).

Sökefeld concludes, "The development of diaspora identity is not simply a natural and inevitable result of migration but a historical contingency that frequently develops out of mobilization in response to specific critical events" (2006, P. 280). Carter (2005) similarly asserts, "[New] Diaspora is now conceived together with a range of other concepts (hybridity, nomadism, creolization) that seek to celebrate the progressive potential of such positions, to overcome the fixed and essentialized assumptions regarding both identity and territory" (P. 55). It is within this (transnational) expanded and less restrictive characterization of diaspora that cultural identity-based diasporic mobilization occurs, which is not necessarily rooted in a location-oriented consciousness. Feron (2012) identifies a new framework and various factors that impact diasporic community organizations and the activities that mobilize the greater diasporic population, including cultural factors, political aspects of the host country, and social factors relating to the resettlement process. Feron notes that a majority of diasporic members relocate to democratic countries, which allows them more resources and time to devote to understanding and spreading awareness of conflicts (and politics in the home and host country).

In terms of political factors, Feron argues that members of diaspora must cope with a major shift in thinking, going from a political majority (often) in the homeland, to political minorities in the host country. Political uncertainty also arises as many within diasporic communities may not be accustomed to free political participation or protected rights, such as free speech and assembly. The diasporic community may also face personal conflict as the host society's politics may differ greatly from their homeland, causing a possible shift of political ideologies and traditional political thought. As Werbner (2002, P. 126) argues, "No longer defined as permanent strangers, they [diasporic populations] expect as a right to be granted full citizenship in their country of settlement. They have become, in a sense, also *ethnics*", which highlights the uncertainty discussed previously. Socially, as highlighted in the Chapter Four interviews, many members of diasporic communities face social upheaval in host societies in relation to employment, socializing or finding companions in a new place as the Other, even mundane activities such as grocery shopping can be difficult when you are obviously different than native citizens. Diasporic members may feel pressured to assimilate into the wider host society and adopt host country traditions and norms, producing a sense of losing one's sense of original identity. Danforth argues,

*If national minorities choose to resist assimilation and retain, or more properly, construct, their own histories, cultures and identities, they must do so without the vast array of facilities that are available to the state, such as national universities, state primary schools, standardized print languages, and ceremonies of national independence. (1996, P. 22)*

As Feron concludes, "Diaspora groups are socialized and confronted with new cultural schemes, which they consciously and unconsciously integrate and mingle with their own 'traditional' cultural schemes; second, such a hybridization seems unavoidable if they wish to ease their political and social integration within host society" (2012, P. 23). Thus the concept of transnational citizenship does come with downsides that must be negotiated by the diasporic community repeatedly over the course of its existence. However, that negotiation and re-negotiation has become relatively easier and more effective in terms of mobilization in the digital age. Diasporas (and other political phenomena such as social movements) are now occurring in a globalized, digital, transnational environment that emphasizes both the local and international politics simultaneously. The future of research on diaspora politics needs to adapt to the incorporation of digital technologies in the establishment and sustainability of diasporic communities across the world.

As the international community (thus diasporic communities within it) has become more interconnected, interdependent, and increasingly more aware of self, society, and heritage – diasporic communities are able to establish and sustain the collective identity over time via digital technologies. These tools, including the internet, social media platforms, and various other mediums of communication have the potential to construct and maintain diasporic networks and the ever-important dialogue where the characterizations and definitions of diaspora are negotiated and reproduced. The availability and increasing use of digital media to maintain diasporic communities allows for the proliferation and solidification of diasporic political, social, and cultural ideologies, which can lead to the fomenting of dispersed migrants into an organized and mobilized transnational diaspora.

## REFERENCES

Adamson, F. (2016). The Growing Importance of Diaspora Politics. *Current History (New York, N.Y.)*, *115*(784), 291–297.

Carter, S. (2005). The Geopolitics of Diaspora. *Area*, *37*(1), 54–63. doi:10.1111/j.1475-4762.2005.00601.x

Cho, L. (2007). The Turn to Diaspora. *Topia*, *17*, 11–30. doi:10.3138/topia.17.11

Cohen, R. (1997/2008). *Global Diasporas: An Introduction*. London: University College London Press. doi:10.4324/9780203228920

Danforth, L. (1996). *The Macedonian Conflict: Ethnic Nationalism in a Transnational World*. Princeton, NJ: Princeton University Press.

Feron, E. (2012). Diaspora Politics: from long distance nationalism to autonomization. In D. Halm & Z. Sezgin (Eds.), *Migration and Organized Civil Society: Rethinking National Policy*. London: Routledge.

Koopmans, R., & Statham, P. (2002). How National Citizenship Shapes Transnationalism: A Comparative Analysis of Migrant and Minority Claims-Making in Germany, Great Britain and the Netherlands. In C. Joppke & E. Morawska (Eds.), *Towards Assimilation and Citizenship: Immigrants in Liberal Nation-States*. London: Palgrave.

Mandaville, P. (2001). Reimagining Islam in Diaspora: The Politics of Mediated Community. *Gazette*, *63*(2–3), 169–186. doi:10.1177/0016549201063002005

Sökefeld, M. (2006). Mobilizing in transnational space: A social movement approach to the formation of diaspora. *Global Networks*, *6*(3), 265–284. doi:10.1111/j.1471-0374.2006.00144.x

Vertovec, S. (1999). Conceiving and researching transnationalism. *Ethnic and Racial Studies*, *22*(2), 447–462. doi:10.1080/014198799329558

Werbner, P. (2002). The place which is diaspora: Citizenship, religion and gender in the making of chaordic transnationalism. *Journal of Ethnic and Migration Studies*, *28*(1), 119–134. doi:10.1080/13691830120103967

# Related Readings

To continue IGI Global's long-standing tradition of advancing innovation through emerging research, please find below a compiled list of recommended IGI Global book chapters and journal articles in the areas of global diaspora, gender movement, and nationalism. These related readings will provide additional information and guidance to further enrich your knowledge and assist you with your own research.

Abereijo, I. O., & Afolabi, J. F. (2017). Religiosity and Entrepreneurship Intentions among Pentecostal Christians. In S. Ojo (Ed.), *Diasporas and Transnational Entrepreneurship in Global Contexts* (pp. 236–251). Hershey, PA: IGI Global. doi:10.4018/978-1-5225-1991-1.ch014

Afolabi, J. F., & Abereijo, I. O. (2017). Returnee Entrepreneurship and Occupational Health and Safety in Nigeria. In S. Ojo (Ed.), *Diasporas and Transnational Entrepreneurship in Global Contexts* (pp. 90–101). Hershey, PA: IGI Global. doi:10.4018/978-1-5225-1991-1.ch005

Ahmed, Z. S. (2018). The Syrian Refugee Crisis and the Role of the Organization of Islamic Cooperation (OIC). In C. Akrivopoulou (Ed.), *Global Perspectives on Human Migration, Asylum, and Security* (pp. 115–126). Hershey, PA: IGI Global. doi:10.4018/978-1-5225-2817-3.ch006

Ahuja, D. (2018). Child Labour: Psychological and Behavioral Challenges. In S. Chhabra (Ed.), *Handbook of Research on Civic Engagement and Social Change in Contemporary Society* (pp. 238–252). Hershey, PA: IGI Global. doi:10.4018/978-1-5225-4197-4.ch014

Arthur, T. (2016). Nollywood Afrogeeks: Nigerian Cinema, Digital Diasporas, and African Immigrants in the United States. *International Journal of E-Politics, 7*(3), 49–64. doi:10.4018/IJEP.2016070104

Azad, S. K. (2016). Women, Migration, Ready Made Garment Factories in Dhaka: Formation of New Class, Culture, and Relationships? In N. Mahtab, S. Parker, F. Kabir, T. Haque, A. Sabur, & A. Sowad (Eds.), *Revealing Gender Inequalities and Perceptions in South Asian Countries through Discourse Analysis* (pp. 41–56). Hershey, PA: IGI Global. doi:10.4018/978-1-5225-0279-1.ch003

Baran, A. G. (2018). Through the Syrians Refuge in Turkey Towards the Creation of the War Migration Theory. In Ş. Erçetin (Ed.), *Social Considerations of Migration Movements and Immigration Policies* (pp. 178–196). Hershey, PA: IGI Global. doi:10.4018/978-1-5225-3322-1.ch011

Bhattacharyya, D. K. (2016). Effectiveness of Critical Discourse Analysis to Solve Constrained Employment Relations: Application Based Study on Two Indian Organizations. In N. Mahtab, S. Parker, F. Kabir, T. Haque, A. Sabur, & A. Sowad (Eds.), *Revealing Gender Inequalities and Perceptions in South Asian Countries through Discourse Analysis* (pp. 100–120). Hershey, PA: IGI Global. doi:10.4018/978-1-5225-0279-1.ch006

Brahmana, R., & Chen, S. (2016). The Role of Women Directors for Malaysian Firms' Performance. In N. Mahtab, S. Parker, F. Kabir, T. Haque, A. Sabur, & A. Sowad (Eds.), *Revealing Gender Inequalities and Perceptions in South Asian Countries through Discourse Analysis* (pp. 121–136). Hershey, PA: IGI Global. doi:10.4018/978-1-5225-0279-1.ch007

Brice, T. S. (2016). Race Relations in the Churches of Christ: Strategies towards Reconciliation. In B. Glimps & T. Ford (Eds.), *Gender and Diversity Issues in Religious-Based Institutions and Organizations* (pp. 184–199). Hershey, PA: IGI Global. doi:10.4018/978-1-4666-8772-1.ch008

Briziarelli, M., & Flores, J. (2018). Mediation Is the Message: Social Media Ventures in Informational Capitalism. In S. Chhabra (Ed.), *Handbook of Research on Civic Engagement and Social Change in Contemporary Society* (pp. 311–327). Hershey, PA: IGI Global. doi:10.4018/978-1-5225-4197-4.ch018

Calvain, E. F. (2018). LGBT Right Activism and the Risk of Christianophobia in Nigeria. In C. Akrivopoulou (Ed.), *Global Perspectives on Human Migration, Asylum, and Security* (pp. 143–165). Hershey, PA: IGI Global. doi:10.4018/978-1-5225-2817-3.ch008

Çelik, S. (2018). Evaluation of the Migration Phenomenon as an Economics Dimension. In Ş. Erçetin (Ed.), *Social Considerations of Migration Movements and Immigration Policies* (pp. 58–65). Hershey, PA: IGI Global. doi:10.4018/978-1-5225-3322-1.ch004

Chapman, C. (2018). Student Acceptance of a Civic Engagement Graduation Requirement in an Urban Community College. In S. Chhabra (Ed.), *Handbook of Research on Civic Engagement and Social Change in Contemporary Society* (pp. 40–62). Hershey, PA: IGI Global. doi:10.4018/978-1-5225-4197-4.ch003

Chhabra, S. (2018). Framework for Enhancing Organizational Performance: Haryana Government Departments, India. In S. Chhabra (Ed.), *Handbook of Research on Civic Engagement and Social Change in Contemporary Society* (pp. 169–182). Hershey, PA: IGI Global. doi:10.4018/978-1-5225-4197-4.ch010

Chowdhury, F. (2016). Permanently Temporary: The Production of Race, Class, and Gender Hierarchies through a Study of Canada's Temporary Foreign Worker Program. In N. Mahtab, S. Parker, F. Kabir, T. Haque, A. Sabur, & A. Sowad (Eds.), *Discourse Analysis as a Tool for Understanding Gender Identity, Representation, and Equality* (pp. 175–203). Hershey, PA: IGI Global. doi:10.4018/978-1-5225-0225-8.ch009

Çolakoğlu, E., & Gök, G. (2018). The Politics of Humanitarian Aid and Civil Protection Policies for Refugees in the Erzurum City of Turkey. In Ş. Erçetin (Ed.), *Social Considerations of Migration Movements and Immigration Policies* (pp. 197–215). Hershey, PA: IGI Global. doi:10.4018/978-1-5225-3322-1.ch012

De Moraes, A. J., Ekanem, I., & Osabutey, E. (2017). New Perspectives on the Internationalisation of Micro-Businesses. In S. Ojo (Ed.), *Diasporas and Transnational Entrepreneurship in Global Contexts* (pp. 115–129). Hershey, PA: IGI Global. doi:10.4018/978-1-5225-1991-1.ch007

Dhoest, A. (2016). Feeling (Dis)Connected: Diasporic LGBTQs and Digital Media. *International Journal of E-Politics*, *7*(3), 35–48. doi:10.4018/IJEP.2016070103

Doğru, Ç. (2018). An Insight into Global Perspectives on Human Resources Management Practices for Immigrants and Refugees. In Ş. Erçetin (Ed.), *Social Considerations of Migration Movements and Immigration Policies* (pp. 102–116). Hershey, PA: IGI Global. doi:10.4018/978-1-5225-3322-1.ch007

Domboka, T. (2017). The Migration History of Black Africans to Britain. In S. Ojo (Ed.), *Diasporas and Transnational Entrepreneurship in Global Contexts* (pp. 188–204). Hershey, PA: IGI Global. doi:10.4018/978-1-5225-1991-1.ch011

Ekanem, I., & Uwajeh, N. J. (2017). Transnational Entrepreneurs and Their Global Market Entry Modes. In S. Ojo (Ed.), *Diasporas and Transnational Entrepreneurship in Global Contexts* (pp. 130–151). Hershey, PA: IGI Global. doi:10.4018/978-1-5225-1991-1.ch008

Elo, M. (2017). Understanding Transnational Diaspora Entrepreneurship and the Role of Values. In S. Ojo (Ed.), *Diasporas and Transnational Entrepreneurship in Global Contexts* (pp. 45–65). Hershey, PA: IGI Global. doi:10.4018/978-1-5225-1991-1.ch003

Eminoğlu, C. (2018). Dispersion, Diaspora Identity and Belonging: A Case Study on the Turkish Migrants in Copenhagen. In Ş. Erçetin (Ed.), *Social Considerations of Migration Movements and Immigration Policies* (pp. 66–82). Hershey, PA: IGI Global. doi:10.4018/978-1-5225-3322-1.ch005

Eraso, A. B., & Cid, D. D. (2016). The Role of Women in the Development of New Religious Movements in Latin America: The Case of Pentecostalism. In B. Glimps & T. Ford (Eds.), *Gender and Diversity Issues in Religious-Based Institutions and Organizations* (pp. 224–247). Hershey, PA: IGI Global. doi:10.4018/978-1-4666-8772-1.ch010

Erçetin, Ş. Ş., & Bisaso, S. M. (2018). Staff Development Programs in the Wake of Migration and Refugee Crisis. In Ş. Erçetin (Ed.), *Social Considerations of Migration Movements and Immigration Policies* (pp. 83–101). Hershey, PA: IGI Global. doi:10.4018/978-1-5225-3322-1.ch006

Erçetin, Ş. Ş., Potas, N., Açıkalın, Ş. N., Özdemir, N., & Doğan, A. M. (2018). Municipalities and Refugee Crisis: Ansar Policies and Numbers. In Ş. Erçetin (Ed.), *Social Considerations of Migration Movements and Immigration Policies* (pp. 46–57). Hershey, PA: IGI Global. doi:10.4018/978-1-5225-3322-1.ch003

Ertaş, B. (2018). I Am Safe While Playing. I Know You Feel the Same Emotions. In Ş. Erçetin (Ed.), *Social Considerations of Migration Movements and Immigration Policies* (pp. 231–247). Hershey, PA: IGI Global. doi:10.4018/978-1-5225-3322-1.ch014

Essien, E. D. (2018). Strengthening Performance of Civil Society Through Dialogue and Critical Thinking in Nigeria: Its Ethical Implications. In S. Chhabra (Ed.), *Handbook of Research on Civic Engagement and Social Change in Contemporary Society* (pp. 82–102). Hershey, PA: IGI Global. doi:10.4018/978-1-5225-4197-4.ch005

Fanaian, T. (2017). The Theocratic Deception Trap: Khomeini's Persuasion Techniques and Communication Patterns in His Books, Guardianship of the Jurist 1979 and Testament 1989. In E. Lewin, E. Bick, & D. Naor (Eds.), *Comparative Perspectives on Civil Religion, Nationalism, and Political Influence* (pp. 62–105). Hershey, PA: IGI Global. doi:10.4018/978-1-5225-0516-7.ch003

Ferdowsi, L. (2016). Intersections of Gender, Sex, and Power: Control over Women's Bodies and Sexuality Amongst the Bangladeshi Diaspora in Britain. In N. Mahtab, S. Parker, F. Kabir, T. Haque, A. Sabur, & A. Sowad (Eds.), *Discourse Analysis as a Tool for Understanding Gender Identity, Representation, and Equality* (pp. 1–24). Hershey, PA: IGI Global. doi:10.4018/978-1-5225-0225-8.ch001

Fındık, L. Y. (2018). Is Turkey Well Prepared for the Integration of Immigrants? In Ş. Erçetin (Ed.), *Social Considerations of Migration Movements and Immigration Policies* (pp. 216–230). Hershey, PA: IGI Global. doi:10.4018/978-1-5225-3322-1.ch013

Fisherman, S. (2016). Body Image and Wellbeing in Religious Male and Female Youth in Israel: An Educational Challenge. In B. Glimps & T. Ford (Eds.), *Gender and Diversity Issues in Religious-Based Institutions and Organizations* (pp. 51–79). Hershey, PA: IGI Global. doi:10.4018/978-1-4666-8772-1.ch003

Ford, T. N., & Glimps, B. J. (2016). A Comparison of "Inclusiveness" in Two Liberal Arts Catholic Universities: What Nurtures an Inclusive Campus Climate? In B. Glimps & T. Ford (Eds.), *Gender and Diversity Issues in Religious-Based Institutions and Organizations* (pp. 159–183). Hershey, PA: IGI Global. doi:10.4018/978-1-4666-8772-1.ch007

Gillath, N. (2017). Avoiding Conscription in Israel: Were Women Pawns in the Political Game? In E. Lewin, E. Bick, & D. Naor (Eds.), *Comparative Perspectives on Civil Religion, Nationalism, and Political Influence* (pp. 226–256). Hershey, PA: IGI Global. doi:10.4018/978-1-5225-0516-7.ch009

Güler, A. (2018). PKK-Related Asylum Applications from Turkey: Counter-Terrorism Measures vs. Refugee Status. In Ş. Erçetin (Ed.), *Social Considerations of Migration Movements and Immigration Policies* (pp. 117–142). Hershey, PA: IGI Global. doi:10.4018/978-1-5225-3322-1.ch008

Gürkan, H. (2017). Migration and Alienation: "When and Where Have I Changed?" – An Analysis through Turkey-Austrian Migration Film. In S. Ojo (Ed.), *Diasporas and Transnational Entrepreneurship in Global Contexts* (pp. 205–218). Hershey, PA: IGI Global. doi:10.4018/978-1-5225-1991-1.ch012

Gurpinar, B. (2018). Supporter, Activist, Rebel, Terrorist: Children in Syria. In C. Akrivopoulou (Ed.), *Global Perspectives on Human Migration, Asylum, and Security* (pp. 97–114). Hershey, PA: IGI Global. doi:10.4018/978-1-5225-2817-3.ch005

Harris-Smith, Y. J. (2016). Spiritual Health Identity: Placing Black Women's Lives in the Center of Analysis. In B. Glimps & T. Ford (Eds.), *Gender and Diversity Issues in Religious-Based Institutions and Organizations* (pp. 1–23). Hershey, PA: IGI Global. doi:10.4018/978-1-4666-8772-1.ch001

Henama, U. S., & Sifolo, P. P. (2017). Tourism Migration in South Africa: Current Dynamics, Immediate Challenges and Future Prospects. *International Journal of Innovation in the Digital Economy*, *8*(1), 47–60. doi:10.4018/IJIDE.2017010103

Higgs, E. T. (2016). Becoming 'Multi-Racial': The Young Women's Christian Association in Kenya, 1955-1965. In B. Glimps & T. Ford (Eds.), *Gender and Diversity Issues in Religious-Based Institutions and Organizations* (pp. 24–50). Hershey, PA: IGI Global. doi:10.4018/978-1-4666-8772-1.ch002

Hosain, J. (2016). Beauty, Choice, and Empowerment: Does Cosmetic Surgery Translate into Gendered Empowerment in Bangladesh? In N. Mahtab, S. Parker, F. Kabir, T. Haque, A. Sabur, & A. Sowad (Eds.), *Revealing Gender Inequalities and Perceptions in South Asian Countries through Discourse Analysis* (pp. 191–207). Hershey, PA: IGI Global. doi:10.4018/978-1-5225-0279-1.ch011

Huang, Q., Osabutey, E. L., Ji, J., & Meng, L. (2017). The Impact of Social Networks on "Born Globals": A Case of De-Internationalisation. In S. Ojo (Ed.), *Diasporas and Transnational Entrepreneurship in Global Contexts* (pp. 152–172). Hershey, PA: IGI Global. doi:10.4018/978-1-5225-1991-1.ch009

Igah, F. (2016). Changing the Traditional Education of Igbo Females: The Role of Religion in Colonial Education. In B. Glimps & T. Ford (Eds.), *Gender and Diversity Issues in Religious-Based Institutions and Organizations* (pp. 291–305). Hershey, PA: IGI Global. doi:10.4018/978-1-4666-8772-1.ch013

Ihebuzor, N., & Egbunike, N. A. (2018). Fencism: An Unusual Political Alignment in Twitter Nigeria. In S. Chhabra (Ed.), *Handbook of Research on Civic Engagement and Social Change in Contemporary Society* (pp. 364–382). Hershey, PA: IGI Global. doi:10.4018/978-1-5225-4197-4.ch021

Islam, A. (2016). Disparity between Boys and Girls: Concerning Sports in Secondary Level Academic Institutions. In N. Mahtab, S. Parker, F. Kabir, T. Haque, A. Sabur, & A. Sowad (Eds.), *Discourse Analysis as a Tool for Understanding Gender Identity, Representation, and Equality* (pp. 157–174). Hershey, PA: IGI Global. doi:10.4018/978-1-5225-0225-8.ch008

Jabin, M. (2016). Struggle against ICT-Based Violence: Locating Socialization Process of Young Men as a Hidden Cause of Women's Vulnerability. In N. Mahtab, S. Parker, F. Kabir, T. Haque, A. Sabur, & A. Sowad (Eds.), *Discourse Analysis as a Tool for Understanding Gender Identity, Representation, and Equality* (pp. 218–235). Hershey, PA: IGI Global. doi:10.4018/978-1-5225-0225-8.ch011

Jahan, F., Wahab, S. A., & Hafiz, F. B. (2016). Gender and Ethnic Discrimination: Life of Mainstream and Indigenous Women in Bangladesh. In N. Mahtab, S. Parker, F. Kabir, T. Haque, A. Sabur, & A. Sowad (Eds.), *Revealing Gender Inequalities and Perceptions in South Asian Countries through Discourse Analysis* (pp. 148–163). Hershey, PA: IGI Global. doi:10.4018/978-1-5225-0279-1.ch009

Jahan, F. R. (2016). Agency, Gender Identities, and Clothing Consumption: The Discourse on Garment Workers. In N. Mahtab, S. Parker, F. Kabir, T. Haque, A. Sabur, & A. Sowad (Eds.), *Discourse Analysis as a Tool for Understanding Gender Identity, Representation, and Equality* (pp. 136–156). Hershey, PA: IGI Global. doi:10.4018/978-1-5225-0225-8.ch007

Joshi, N. (2016). Urban Nepali Women and Experiences of Love, Intimate Relations, and Media. In N. Mahtab, S. Parker, F. Kabir, T. Haque, A. Sabur, & A. Sowad (Eds.), *Revealing Gender Inequalities and Perceptions in South Asian Countries through Discourse Analysis* (pp. 20–40). Hershey, PA: IGI Global. doi:10.4018/978-1-5225-0279-1.ch002

Kalagy, T. (2017). Values, Constraints, and Maneuvers: Processes of Academization among Ultra-Orthodox Women and Beduin Women in Israel. In E. Lewin, E. Bick, & D. Naor (Eds.), *Comparative Perspectives on Civil Religion, Nationalism, and Political Influence* (pp. 257–284). Hershey, PA: IGI Global. doi:10.4018/978-1-5225-0516-7.ch010

Karamagioli, E., Staiou, E. R., & Gouscos, D. (2018). Assessing the Social Media Presence and Activity of Major Greek Cities During 2014-2017: Towards Local Government 2.0? In S. Chhabra (Ed.), *Handbook of Research on Civic Engagement and Social Change in Contemporary Society* (pp. 272–293). Hershey, PA: IGI Global. doi:10.4018/978-1-5225-4197-4.ch016

Kasemsap, K. (2017). Entrepreneurship and Diaspora Entrepreneurship: Current Issues and Approaches. In S. Ojo (Ed.), *Diasporas and Transnational Entrepreneurship in Global Contexts* (pp. 23–44). Hershey, PA: IGI Global. doi:10.4018/978-1-5225-1991-1.ch002

Kavaklı, N. (2018). Hate Speech Towards Syrian Refugees in Turkish Online Reader Comments. In C. Akrivopoulou (Ed.), *Global Perspectives on Human Migration, Asylum, and Security* (pp. 127–142). Hershey, PA: IGI Global. doi:10.4018/978-1-5225-2817-3.ch007

Khan, M. (2016). Implications of Citizenship Discourse on Female Labour Force Participation: A Case Study of Bangladeshi Women in the UK. In N. Mahtab, S. Parker, F. Kabir, T. Haque, A. Sabur, & A. Sowad (Eds.), *Discourse Analysis as a Tool for Understanding Gender Identity, Representation, and Equality* (pp. 25–49). Hershey, PA: IGI Global. doi:10.4018/978-1-5225-0225-8.ch002

Khan, M. M., & Ara, F. (2016). Women in Bangladesh Local Government: Critically Evaluating Their Participation and Empowerment. In N. Mahtab, S. Parker, F. Kabir, T. Haque, A. Sabur, & A. Sowad (Eds.), *Revealing Gender Inequalities and Perceptions in South Asian Countries through Discourse Analysis* (pp. 80–99). Hershey, PA: IGI Global. doi:10.4018/978-1-5225-0279-1.ch005

Khanum, R. A. (2016). Equality and Differences: Some Feminist Thoughts. In N. Mahtab, S. Parker, F. Kabir, T. Haque, A. Sabur, & A. Sowad (Eds.), *Discourse Analysis as a Tool for Understanding Gender Identity, Representation, and Equality* (pp. 204–217). Hershey, PA: IGI Global. doi:10.4018/978-1-5225-0225-8.ch010

Kim, Y. K., Edens, D., Parra, O. E., & Lopez, K. M. (2016). Sense of Belonging in Religious-Based Colleges and Universities: Predictors and Patterns among Students of Color and White Students. In B. Glimps & T. Ford (Eds.), *Gender and Diversity Issues in Religious-Based Institutions and Organizations* (pp. 269–290). Hershey, PA: IGI Global. doi:10.4018/978-1-4666-8772-1.ch012

Korstanje, M. E. (2018). How Can World Leaders Understand the Perverse Core of Terrorism?: Terror in the Global Village. In C. Akrivopoulou (Ed.), *Global Perspectives on Human Migration, Asylum, and Security* (pp. 48–67). Hershey, PA: IGI Global. doi:10.4018/978-1-5225-2817-3.ch003

Korstanje, M. E. (2018). Thana-Capitalism and the Sense of Reality: Lessons Unlearned. In C. Akrivopoulou (Ed.), *Global Perspectives on Human Migration, Asylum, and Security* (pp. 1–20). Hershey, PA: IGI Global. doi:10.4018/978-1-5225-2817-3.ch001

Lawler, J. A., & Mir, G. (2016). Women, Faith, and Social Cohesion. In B. Glimps & T. Ford (Eds.), *Gender and Diversity Issues in Religious-Based Institutions and Organizations* (pp. 200–223). Hershey, PA: IGI Global. doi:10.4018/978-1-4666-8772-1.ch009

Leocadia, D. R. (2018). The Use of Social Media by Local Governments: Benefits, Challenges, and Recent Experiences. In S. Chhabra (Ed.), *Handbook of Research on Civic Engagement and Social Change in Contemporary Society* (pp. 294–310). Hershey, PA: IGI Global. doi:10.4018/978-1-5225-4197-4.ch017

Leon, N. (2017). The Haredi Scholar-Society and the Military Draft in Israel: Counter-Nationalism and the Imagined Military Symbiosis. In E. Lewin, E. Bick, & D. Naor (Eds.), *Comparative Perspectives on Civil Religion, Nationalism, and Political Influence* (pp. 210–225). Hershey, PA: IGI Global. doi:10.4018/978-1-5225-0516-7.ch008

Leurs, K. (2016). Young Connected Migrants and Non-Normative European Family Life: Exploring Affective Human Right Claims of Young E-Diasporas. *International Journal of E-Politics, 7*(3), 15–34. doi:10.4018/IJEP.2016070102

Lewin, E., & Bick, E. (2017). Introduction: Civil Religion and Nationalism on a Godly-Civil Continuum. In E. Lewin, E. Bick, & D. Naor (Eds.), *Comparative Perspectives on Civil Religion, Nationalism, and Political Influence* (pp. 1–31). Hershey, PA: IGI Global. doi:10.4018/978-1-5225-0516-7.ch001

Marques, B., McIntosh, J., & Campays, P. (2018). Participatory Design for Under-Represented Communities: A Collaborative Design-Led Research Approach for Place-Making. In S. Chhabra (Ed.), *Handbook of Research on Civic Engagement and Social Change in Contemporary Society* (pp. 1–15). Hershey, PA: IGI Global. doi:10.4018/978-1-5225-4197-4.ch001

Matiatou, M. (2018). NGOs, Civil Society, and Global Governance in the Era of Sustainability and Consolidation: A Taxonomy of Value. In S. Chhabra (Ed.), *Handbook of Research on Civic Engagement and Social Change in Contemporary Society* (pp. 183–206). Hershey, PA: IGI Global. doi:10.4018/978-1-5225-4197-4.ch011

McCarthy-Latimer, C. (2018). Higher Education Pedagogy Revisited: Impacting Political Science College Students' Active Learning, Opinion Development, and Participation. In S. Chhabra (Ed.), *Handbook of Research on Civic Engagement and Social Change in Contemporary Society* (pp. 63–81). Hershey, PA: IGI Global. doi:10.4018/978-1-5225-4197-4.ch004

Menteşe, M. (2018). Social Capital and Immigrants. In Ş. Erçetin (Ed.), *Social Considerations of Migration Movements and Immigration Policies* (pp. 143–153). Hershey, PA: IGI Global. doi:10.4018/978-1-5225-3322-1.ch009

Mutanda, D. (2018). Peace Building Lessons from the Civilian Survival Strategy of Flight in Syria, 2011-2016. In Ş. Erçetin (Ed.), *Social Considerations of Migration Movements and Immigration Policies* (pp. 154–177). Hershey, PA: IGI Global. doi:10.4018/978-1-5225-3322-1.ch010

Nayak, S. (2018). Agriculture Livelihood Security: Industry CSR Initiative. In S. Chhabra (Ed.), *Handbook of Research on Civic Engagement and Social Change in Contemporary Society* (pp. 103–118). Hershey, PA: IGI Global. doi:10.4018/978-1-5225-4197-4.ch006

Ndhlovu, T. P., & Ndinda, C. (2017). Social Entrepreneurship in Sub-Saharan Africa: A Critical Analysis of Diaspora Social Investments. In S. Ojo (Ed.), *Diasporas and Transnational Entrepreneurship in Global Contexts* (pp. 219–235). Hershey, PA: IGI Global. doi:10.4018/978-1-5225-1991-1.ch013

Neugröschel, M. (2017). Anti-Semitism as a Civil Religion: Progressive Paradigms in the Anti-Semitic Construction of German National Identity. In E. Lewin, E. Bick, & D. Naor (Eds.), *Comparative Perspectives on Civil Religion, Nationalism, and Political Influence* (pp. 106–124). Hershey, PA: IGI Global. doi:10.4018/978-1-5225-0516-7.ch004

Ojo, E. I. (2017). Returnee Entrepreneurship: A Second-Generation Perspective. In S. Ojo (Ed.), *Diasporas and Transnational Entrepreneurship in Global Contexts* (pp. 102–114). Hershey, PA: IGI Global. doi:10.4018/978-1-5225-1991-1.ch006

Ojo, S. (2017). Examining the Impact of Symbolic Capital in Ethnic and Diaspora Entrepreneurship. In S. Ojo (Ed.), *Diasporas and Transnational Entrepreneurship in Global Contexts* (pp. 66–89). Hershey, PA: IGI Global. doi:10.4018/978-1-5225-1991-1.ch004

Ojo, S. (2017). The "Gospel" of Pentecostalism and Entrepreneurship: A Market Configuration. In S. Ojo (Ed.), *Diasporas and Transnational Entrepreneurship in Global Contexts* (pp. 252–273). Hershey, PA: IGI Global. doi:10.4018/978-1-5225-1991-1.ch015

Ojo, S., & Nwankwo, S. (2017). Diaspora and Transnational Entrepreneurship: A Conceptual Exploration. In S. Ojo (Ed.), *Diasporas and Transnational Entrepreneurship in Global Contexts* (pp. 1–22). Hershey, PA: IGI Global. doi:10.4018/978-1-5225-1991-1.ch001

Okezie, C. E., Alhamisi, J., & Glimps, B. J. (2016). The Promise for African American Male Students in Teacher Education at Marygrove College. In B. Glimps & T. Ford (Eds.), *Gender and Diversity Issues in Religious-Based Institutions and Organizations* (pp. 137–158). Hershey, PA: IGI Global. doi:10.4018/978-1-4666-8772-1.ch006

Okoya, J. (2017). Interfacing with Diaspora/Ethnic Entrepreneurship: A Case of Getting the Right Balance in the HRM Ethnic Marketing Nexus. In S. Ojo (Ed.), *Diasporas and Transnational Entrepreneurship in Global Contexts* (pp. 173–187). Hershey, PA: IGI Global. doi:10.4018/978-1-5225-1991-1.ch010

Omotosho, B. J. (2017). Situating the Place of Youths' between African Union and Africa Diaspora. *International Journal of Social Ecology and Sustainable Development, 8*(2), 57–67. doi:10.4018/IJSESD.2017040104

Omotosho, B. J. (2018). Reconnoitering the Fight Against Political Corruption and the Way Forward in Nigeria. In S. Chhabra (Ed.), *Handbook of Research on Civic Engagement and Social Change in Contemporary Society* (pp. 207–219). Hershey, PA: IGI Global. doi:10.4018/978-1-5225-4197-4.ch012

Oravec, J. A. (2018). "Don't Be Evil" and Beyond for High Tech Organizations: Ethical Statements and Mottos (and Responsibility). In S. Chhabra (Ed.), *Handbook of Research on Civic Engagement and Social Change in Contemporary Society* (pp. 220–237). Hershey, PA: IGI Global. doi:10.4018/978-1-5225-4197-4.ch013

Parker, S. L., & Standing, K. (2016). Overcoming Intersectional Barriers: Lessons from "Inspirational" Women in Nepal. In N. Mahtab, S. Parker, F. Kabir, T. Haque, A. Sabur, & A. Sowad (Eds.), *Revealing Gender Inequalities and Perceptions in South Asian Countries through Discourse Analysis* (pp. 164–190). Hershey, PA: IGI Global. doi:10.4018/978-1-5225-0279-1.ch010

Parsa, F. (2016). Challenges of Iranian Women to Change the Gender Discriminatory Law. In N. Mahtab, S. Parker, F. Kabir, T. Haque, A. Sabur, & A. Sowad (Eds.), *Discourse Analysis as a Tool for Understanding Gender Identity, Representation, and Equality* (pp. 74–89). Hershey, PA: IGI Global. doi:10.4018/978-1-5225-0225-8.ch004

Peacock, J. S., & Chowdhury, S. A. (2016). The Effect of Colonialism on the Bangladeshi Female Immigrant in Britain. In N. Mahtab, S. Parker, F. Kabir, T. Haque, A. Sabur, & A. Sowad (Eds.), *Discourse Analysis as a Tool for Understanding Gender Identity, Representation, and Equality* (pp. 90–98). Hershey, PA: IGI Global. doi:10.4018/978-1-5225-0225-8.ch005

Pitsou, A. (2018). Refugees or Migrants: Fascistisation and Punishment. In C. Akrivopoulou (Ed.), *Global Perspectives on Human Migration, Asylum, and Security* (pp. 21–47). Hershey, PA: IGI Global. doi:10.4018/978-1-5225-2817-3.ch002

Quental, C., & Gouveia, L. B. (2018). Participation Sphere: A Model and a Framework for Fostering Participation in Organizations. In S. Chhabra (Ed.), *Handbook of Research on Civic Engagement and Social Change in Contemporary Society* (pp. 16–39). Hershey, PA: IGI Global. doi:10.4018/978-1-5225-4197-4.ch002

Raina, R. L., Alam, I., & Siddiqui, F. (2018). Facebook Losing to WhatsApp: The Changing Social Networking Patterns in India. In S. Chhabra (Ed.), *Handbook of Research on Civic Engagement and Social Change in Contemporary Society* (pp. 328–346). Hershey, PA: IGI Global. doi:10.4018/978-1-5225-4197-4.ch019

Randa, I. O. (2018). Leveraging Hybrid Value Chain for Affordable Housing Delivery in the City of Windhoek. In S. Chhabra (Ed.), *Handbook of Research on Civic Engagement and Social Change in Contemporary Society* (pp. 119–141). Hershey, PA: IGI Global. doi:10.4018/978-1-5225-4197-4.ch007

Risam, R. (2016). Diasporizing the Digital Humanities: Displacing the Center and Periphery. *International Journal of E-Politics*, *7*(3), 65–78. doi:10.4018/IJEP.2016070105

Rosy, S. Y., & Islam, M. M. (2016). Communication Process in Family Reinforcing the Gender Differences in Bangladesh. In N. Mahtab, S. Parker, F. Kabir, T. Haque, A. Sabur, & A. Sowad (Eds.), *Revealing Gender Inequalities and Perceptions in South Asian Countries through Discourse Analysis* (pp. 137–147). Hershey, PA: IGI Global. doi:10.4018/978-1-5225-0279-1.ch008

Rumano, M., & Sommers, R. (2016). Navigating the Terrain of Diversity: Lessons and Insights for Religious Institutions and Faculty from Diverse Backgrounds. In B. Glimps & T. Ford (Eds.), *Gender and Diversity Issues in Religious-Based Institutions and Organizations* (pp. 248–268). Hershey, PA: IGI Global. doi:10.4018/978-1-4666-8772-1.ch011

Samya, A. S. (2016). Diversity or Dilemma: The Cry for Social Freedom of MSM People Living in Dhaka City. In N. Mahtab, S. Parker, F. Kabir, T. Haque, A. Sabur, & A. Sowad (Eds.), *Revealing Gender Inequalities and Perceptions in South Asian Countries through Discourse Analysis* (pp. 1–19). Hershey, PA: IGI Global. doi:10.4018/978-1-5225-0279-1.ch001

Sasson, K. (2017). Religion and Politics: A Troubled Relationship in a Volatile World. In E. Lewin, E. Bick, & D. Naor (Eds.), *Comparative Perspectives on Civil Religion, Nationalism, and Political Influence* (pp. 32–61). Hershey, PA: IGI Global. doi:10.4018/978-1-5225-0516-7.ch002

Semali, L. M. (2018). Indigenous Knowledge as Resource to Sustain Self-Employment in Rural Development. In S. Chhabra (Ed.), *Handbook of Research on Civic Engagement and Social Change in Contemporary Society* (pp. 142–158). Hershey, PA: IGI Global. doi:10.4018/978-1-5225-4197-4.ch008

Sheiner, D. Z. (2017). National-Liberty Reflections of the Exodus Myth in Palestine-Israel Print Media Advertisements, 1923-1958. In E. Lewin, E. Bick, & D. Naor (Eds.), *Comparative Perspectives on Civil Religion, Nationalism, and Political Influence* (pp. 190–209). Hershey, PA: IGI Global. doi:10.4018/978-1-5225-0516-7.ch007

Sowad, A. S. (2016). Migration Affecting Masculinities: The Consequences of Migration on the Construction of Masculinities of Migrant Bangladeshi Men Living in the United Kingdom. In N. Mahtab, S. Parker, F. Kabir, T. Haque, A. Sabur, & A. Sowad (Eds.), *Discourse Analysis as a Tool for Understanding Gender Identity, Representation, and Equality* (pp. 50–73). Hershey, PA: IGI Global. doi:10.4018/978-1-5225-0225-8.ch003

Stacey, E. (2018). Networked Protests: A Review of Social Movement Literature and the Hong Kong Umbrella Movement (2017). In S. Chhabra (Ed.), *Handbook of Research on Civic Engagement and Social Change in Contemporary Society* (pp. 347–363). Hershey, PA: IGI Global. doi:10.4018/978-1-5225-4197-4.ch020

Strongman, L. (2018). Understanding Private and Public Partnerships. In S. Chhabra (Ed.), *Handbook of Research on Civic Engagement and Social Change in Contemporary Society* (pp. 159–168). Hershey, PA: IGI Global. doi:10.4018/978-1-5225-4197-4.ch009

Sultana, I. Z. (2016). The Exploitation of Women Workers: Unveiling Capitalism in Bangladeshi Garment Industries. In N. Mahtab, S. Parker, F. Kabir, T. Haque, A. Sabur, & A. Sowad (Eds.), *Revealing Gender Inequalities and Perceptions in South Asian Countries through Discourse Analysis* (pp. 208–222). Hershey, PA: IGI Global. doi:10.4018/978-1-5225-0279-1.ch012

Tanjeem, N. (2016). Social Media and Conformist Voluntarism in the Neoliberal Era: The Case of Rana Plaza Collapse in Savar, Bangladesh. In N. Mahtab, S. Parker, F. Kabir, T. Haque, A. Sabur, & A. Sowad (Eds.), *Revealing Gender Inequalities and Perceptions in South Asian Countries through Discourse Analysis* (pp. 57–79). Hershey, PA: IGI Global. doi:10.4018/978-1-5225-0279-1.ch004

Tanrısever, O. F., & Türkmen, H. S. (2018). The Securitization Theory and Migration: The Case of Russia's Securitization of Europe's Migration Crisis. In Ş. Erçetin (Ed.), *Social Considerations of Migration Movements and Immigration Policies* (pp. 1–12). Hershey, PA: IGI Global. doi:10.4018/978-1-5225-3322-1.ch001

Teper, Y. (2017). How Civic is Russia's New Civil Religion and How Religious is the Church? In E. Lewin, E. Bick, & D. Naor (Eds.), *Comparative Perspectives on Civil Religion, Nationalism, and Political Influence* (pp. 125–155). Hershey, PA: IGI Global. doi:10.4018/978-1-5225-0516-7.ch005

Tran, B. (2016). Culturally Gendered: The Institutionalization of Men and Masculinities in Society and Corporations. In N. Mahtab, S. Parker, F. Kabir, T. Haque, A. Sabur, & A. Sowad (Eds.), *Discourse Analysis as a Tool for Understanding Gender Identity, Representation, and Equality* (pp. 99–135). Hershey, PA: IGI Global. doi:10.4018/978-1-5225-0225-8.ch006

Tsiftzis, Z., & Kynigopoulou, I. (2018). Providente Asylum vs. the Council of Europe: The Case of Greece. In C. Akrivopoulou (Ed.), *Global Perspectives on Human Migration, Asylum, and Security* (pp. 68–96). Hershey, PA: IGI Global. doi:10.4018/978-1-5225-2817-3.ch004

Tuttle, T. M. (2016). Laborare est Orare: Starting a Gay-Straight Alliance at a Rural, Private, Catholic College. In B. Glimps & T. Ford (Eds.), *Gender and Diversity Issues in Religious-Based Institutions and Organizations* (pp. 124–136). Hershey, PA: IGI Global. doi:10.4018/978-1-4666-8772-1.ch005

Tüzünkan, D. (2018). The International Migration Movements and Immigrant Policies From the Ottoman Empire 1299 to Republican Turkey 2016. In Ş. Erçetin (Ed.), *Social Considerations of Migration Movements and Immigration Policies* (pp. 13–45). Hershey, PA: IGI Global. doi:10.4018/978-1-5225-3322-1.ch002

Vij, R. (2018). Do Women Perceive Organizational Culture Differently From Men?: A Case Study of State Bank of India. In S. Chhabra (Ed.), *Handbook of Research on Civic Engagement and Social Change in Contemporary Society* (pp. 253–271). Hershey, PA: IGI Global. doi:10.4018/978-1-5225-4197-4.ch015

Yefet, B. (2017). The Clash of Civil Religions in Post-Revolutionary Egypt. In E. Lewin, E. Bick, & D. Naor (Eds.), *Comparative Perspectives on Civil Religion, Nationalism, and Political Influence* (pp. 156–189). Hershey, PA: IGI Global. doi:10.4018/978-1-5225-0516-7.ch006

Young, S. (2016). Psychological Essentialism: Diversity and the Religious Experience. In B. Glimps & T. Ford (Eds.), *Gender and Diversity Issues in Religious-Based Institutions and Organizations* (pp. 80–123). Hershey, PA: IGI Global. doi:10.4018/978-1-4666-8772-1.ch004

# About the Author

**Emily Stacey** is a Political Science professor. She successfully completed her dissertation defense in November 2016, and will formally graduate from Swansea University (Wales, UK) in Summer 2017. Emily's dissertation research focuses on the necessity of bureaucratization in contemporary social movements, namely those using digital technologies to mobilize and sustain dissent. She has participated in the Digital Methods Initiative at the University of Amsterdam (2013) and the Oxford Internet Institute's Summer Doctoral Program (2014). Emily has published a book chapter as well as a journal article with IGI before this work. Her future research will focus on the use of digital technologies and social media platforms to influence nationalist movements occurring around the world. You can follow Emily on Twitter: @politikphd.

# Index

## M



## N



## P



## R



## S



## T

## Purchase Print, E-Book, or Print + E-Book

IGI Global books can now be purchased from three unique pricing formats: Print Only, E-Book Only, or Print + E-Book. Shipping fees apply.

**www.igi-global.com**

# Recommended Reference Books

ISBN: 978-1-5225-1986-7
© 2017; 309 pp.
List Price: $195

ISBN: 978-1-5225-0813-7
© 2017; 345 pp.
List Price: $190

ISBN: 978-1-5225-2209-6
© 2017; 322 pp.
List Price: $195

ISBN: 978-1-5225-2578-3
© 2018; 296 pp.
List Price: $195

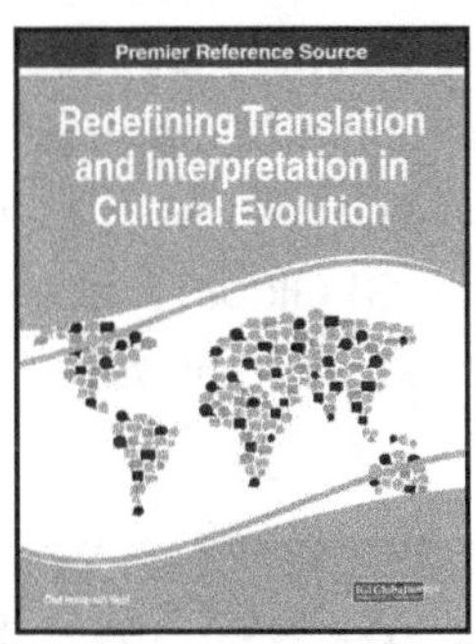


ISBN: 978-1-5225-2832-6
© 2018; 310 pp.
List Price: $195

ISBN: 978-1-5225-3018-3
© 2018; 452 pp.
List Price: $245

**Looking for free content, product updates, news, and special offers?**

Join IGI Global's mailing list today and start enjoying exclusive perks sent only to IGI Global members. Add your name to the list at **www.igi-global.com/newsletters.**

Publisher of Peer-Reviewed, Timely, and Innovative Academic Research

IGI Global
DISSEMINATOR OF KNOWLEDGE

**www.igi-global.com** Sign up at www.igi-global.com/newsletters facebook.com/igiglobal twitter.com/igiglobal

Ensure Quality Research is Introduced to the Academic Community

# Become an IGI Global Reviewer for Authored Book Projects

## The overall success of an authored book project is dependent on quality and timely reviews.

In this competitive age of scholarly publishing, constructive and timely feedback significantly expedites the turnaround time of manuscripts from submission to acceptance, allowing the publication and discovery of forward-thinking research at a much more expeditious rate. Several IGI Global authored book projects are currently seeking highly qualified experts in the field to fill vacancies on their respective editorial review boards:

**Applications may be sent to:**
development@igi-global.com

Applicants must have a doctorate (or an equivalent degree) as well as publishing and reviewing experience. Reviewers are asked to write reviews in a timely, collegial, and constructive manner. All reviewers will begin their role on an ad-hoc basis for a period of one year, and upon successful completion of this term can be considered for full editorial review board status, with the potential for a subsequent promotion to Associate Editor.

If you have a colleague that may be interested in this opportunity, we encourage you to share this information with them.

IGI Global
DISSEMINATOR OF KNOWLEDGE
www.igi-global.com

***Celebrating 30 Years*** of Scholarly Knowledge Creation & Dissemination

# InfoSci®-Books

## A Collection of 4,000+ Reference Books Containing Over 87,000 Full-Text Chapters Focusing on Emerging Research

This database is a collection of over 4,000+ IGI Global single and multi-volume reference books, handbooks of research, and encyclopedias, encompassing groundbreaking research from prominent experts worldwide. These books are highly cited and currently recognized in prestigious indices such as: Web of Science™ and Scopus®.

### Librarian Features:

- No Set-Up or Maintenance Fees
- Guarantee of No More Than A 5% Annual Price Increase
- COUNTER 4 Usage Reports
- Complimentary Archival Access
- Free MARC Records

### Researcher Features:

- Unlimited Simultaneous Users
- No Embargo of Content
- Full Book Download
- Full-Text Search Engine
- No DRM

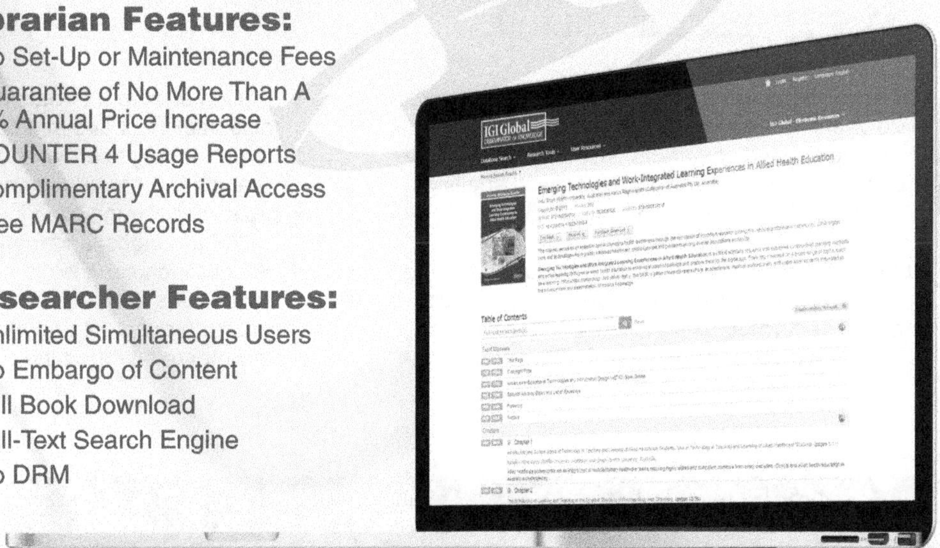


**To Find Out More or To Purchase This Database:**

**www.igi-global.com/infosci-books**

eresources@igi-global.com • Toll Free: 1-866-342-6657 ext. 100 • Phone: 717-533-8845 x100

IGI Global
DISSEMINATOR OF KNOWLEDGE
www.igi-global.com

## IGI Global Proudly Partners with

# eContent Pro International

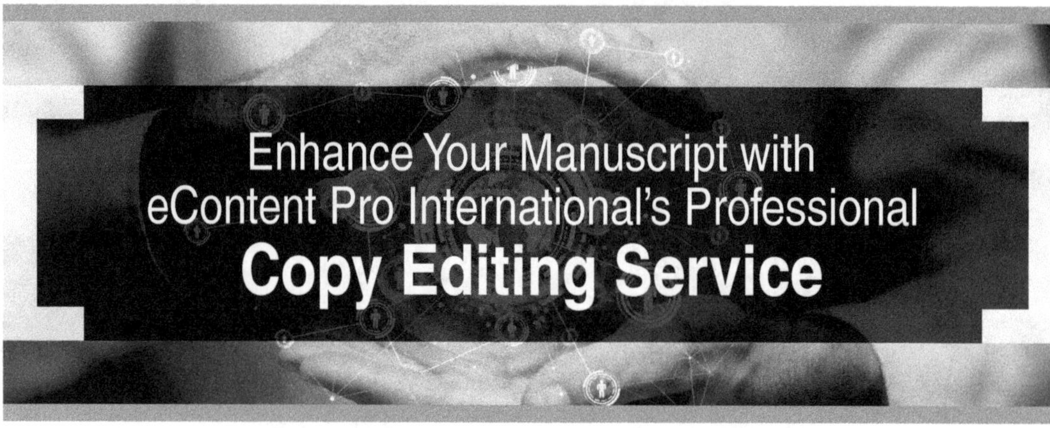


### Expert Copy Editing

eContent Pro International copy editors, with over 70 years of combined experience, will provide complete and comprehensive care for your document by resolving all issues with spelling, punctuation, grammar, terminology, jargon, semantics, syntax, consistency, flow, and more. In addition, they will format your document to the style you specify (APA, Chicago, etc.). All edits will be performed using Microsoft Word's Track Changes feature, which allows for fast and simple review and management of edits.

### Additional Services

eContent Pro International also offers fast and affordable proofreading to enhance the readability of your document, professional translation in over 100 languages, and market localization services to help businesses and organizations localize their content and grow into new markets around the globe.

## IGI Global Authors Save 25% on eContent Pro International's Services!

**Scan the QR Code to Receive Your 25% Discount**

The 25% discount is applied directly to your eContent Pro International shopping cart when placing an order through IGI Global's referral link. Use the QR code to access this referral link. eContent Pro International has the right to end or modify any promotion at any time.

**Email: customerservice@econtentpro.com**

**econtentpro.com**

# Information Resources Management Association

Advancing the Concepts & Practices of Information Resources Management in Modern Organizations

# Become an IRMA Member

Members of the **Information Resources Management Association (IRMA)** understand the importance of community within their field of study. The Information Resources Management Association is an ideal venue through which professionals, students, and academicians can convene and share the latest industry innovations and scholarly research that is changing the field of information science and technology. Become a member today and enjoy the benefits of membership as well as the opportunity to collaborate and network with fellow experts in the field.

## IRMA Membership Benefits:

- **One FREE Journal Subscription**
- **30% Off Additional Journal Subscriptions**
- **20% Off Book Purchases**
- Updates on the latest events and research on Information Resources Management through the IRMA-L listserv.
- Updates on new open access and downloadable content added to Research IRM.
- A copy of the Information Technology Management Newsletter twice a year.
- A certificate of membership.

## IRMA Membership $195

Scan code or visit **irma-international.org** and begin by selecting your free journal subscription.

Membership is good for one full year.

www.irma-international.org

IGI Global
DISSEMINATOR OF KNOWLEDGE
www.igi-global.com

# Available to Order Now

Order through www.igi-global.com with **Free Standard Shipping**.*

## The Premier Reference for Information Science & Information Technology

**100% Original Content**
Contains 705 new, peer-reviewed articles with color figures covering over 80 categories in 11 subject areas

**Diverse Contributions**
More than 1,100 experts from 74 unique countries contributed their specialized knowledge

**Easy Navigation**
Includes two tables of content and a comprehensive index in each volume for the user's convenience

**Highly-Cited**
Embraces a complete list of references and additional reading sections to allow for further research

**Included in:**
InfoSci®-Books

# Encyclopedia of Information Science and Technology Fourth Edition

A Comprehensive 10-Volume Set

**Mehdi Khosrow-Pour, D.B.A.** (Information Resources Management Association, USA)
ISBN: 978-1-5225-2255-3; © 2018; Pg: 8,104; Release Date: July 2017

For a limited time, receive the complimentary e-books for the First, Second, and Third editions with the purchase of the *Encyclopedia of Information Science and Technology, Fourth Edition* e-book.**

The **Encyclopedia of Information Science and Technology, Fourth Edition** is a 10-volume set which includes 705 original and previously unpublished research articles covering a full range of perspectives, applications, and techniques contributed by thousands of experts and researchers from around the globe. This authoritative encyclopedia is an all-encompassing, well-established reference source that is ideally designed to disseminate the most forward-thinking and diverse research findings. With critical perspectives on the impact of information science management and new technologies in modern settings, including but not limited to computer science, education, healthcare, government, engineering, business, and natural and physical sciences, it is a pivotal and relevant source of knowledge that will benefit every professional within the field of information science and technology and is an invaluable addition to every academic and corporate library.

Scan for Online Bookstore

**New Low Pricing!**

Hardcover: **$2,848****
~~List Price: $5,695~~

E-Book: **$2,848****
~~List Price: $5,695~~

Hardcover + E-Book: **$3,448****
~~List Price: $6,895~~

***Both E-Book Prices Include:***

- *Encyclopedia of Information Science and Technology, First Edition E-Book*
- *Encyclopedia of Information Science and Technology, Second Edition E-Book*
- *Encyclopedia of Information Science and Technology, Third Edition E-Book*

*Purchase the Encyclopedia of Information Science and Technology, Fourth Edition e-book and receive the first, second, and third e-book editions for free. Offer is only valid with purchase of the fourth edition's e-book.

**50% discount cannot be combined with any other offer except the free first, second, and third editions e-book offer. Discount is valid on the Encyclopedia of Information Science and Technology, Fourth Edition when purchased directly through the IGI Global Online Bookstore and may not be used by distributors or book sellers.

**Recommend this Title to Your Institution's Library:** www.igi-global.com/books

www.igi-global.com/infosci-ondemand

# InfoSci®-OnDemand

Continuously updated with new material on a weekly basis, InfoSci®-OnDemand offers the ability to search through thousands of quality full-text research papers. Users can narrow each search by identifying key topic areas of interest, then display a complete listing of relevant papers, and purchase materials specific to their research needs.

## Comprehensive Service

- Over 81,600+ journal articles, book chapters, and case studies.
- All content is downloadable in PDF format and can be stored locally for future use.

## No Subscription Fees

- One time fee of **$37.50** per PDF download.

## Instant Access

- Receive a download link immediately after order completion!

"It really provides an excellent entry into the research literature of the field. It presents a manageable number of highly relevant sources on topics of interest to a wide range of researchers. The sources are scholarly, but also accessible to 'practitioners'."

- Lisa Stimatz, MLS, University of North Carolina at Chapel Hill, USA

"It is an excellent and well designed database which will facilitate research, publication and teaching. It is a very very useful tool to have."

- George Ditsa, PhD, University of Wollongong, Australia

"I have accessed the database and find it to be a valuable tool to the IT/IS community. I found valuable articles meeting my search criteria 95% of the time."

- Lynda Louis, Xavier University of Louisiana, USA

**Recommended for use by researchers who wish to immediately download PDFs of individual chapters or articles.**

www.igi-global.com/e-resources/infosci-ondemand

IGI Global DISSEMINATOR OF KNOWLEDGE

www.igi-global.com

www.ingramcontent.com/pod-product-compliance
Lightning Source LLC
LaVergne TN
LVHW062125200926
848484LV00007B/1767